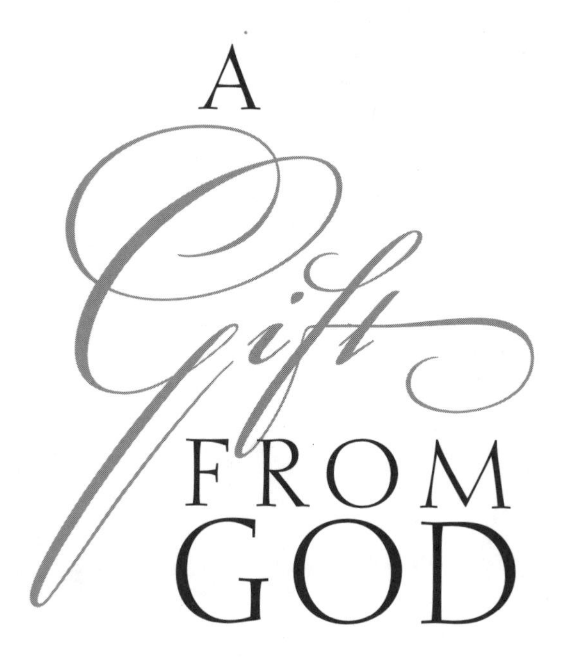
A
Gift
FROM
GOD

JK

FOUNDATIONAL PRINCIPLES OF BIBLICAL PARENTING

A Gift From God

LARRY MERCER

MOODY PRESS
CHICAGO

The poem, "Fragile: Handle with Care," by Ruth Senter, published in *Campus Life,* January/February 2001, is used by permission of the author.

Library of Congress Cataloging-in-Publication Data

Mercer, Larry.
A gift from God : foundational principles of biblical parenting / Larry Mercer.
p. cm.
Includes bibliographical references.
ISBN 0-8024-1441-9
1. Parenting—Religious aspects—Christianity. 2. Parenting—Biblical teaching. I. Title.

BV4529 .M43 2001
248.8'45—dc21

2001030442

1 3 5 7 9 10 8 6 4 2

Printed in the United States of America

There is no competition for who should be the focus of dedication for this book. On a human level, my family has been my greatest teachers, supporters, and cheerleaders. This book could not have happened without the lessons I have learned from them as well as their support and encouragement.

Annie, my dear wife for more than twenty-three years, best friend in the world, and my hero, was the "wind beneath my wings." She has encouraged me to go on at times when it seemed easier to stop. God gave her to me as a great expression of His love for me and I will be eternally grateful.

My children, Timothy, Christopher, Michele, and Anita-Grace, have offered their hands, prayers, and lives to make this project a reality. They have all sacrificed precious parts of their lives to allow this book to finally materialize. We have all grown together, and continue to learn meaningful life lessons, as a result of the lessons we are learning from life.

Finally, my Lord and Savior Jesus Christ deserves any praise and glory that comes as a result of this project now and in the future. And ultimately any glory that comes from this work is dedicated to Him.

CONTENTS

LIST OF PARENTING INSIGHTS

FOREWORD

Babies are a promise of tomorrow, new beginnings, and evidence that the world will keep going—in short, *A Gift from God.* Ever since Eve exclaimed, "With the help of the Lord I have brought forth a son" (Genesis 4:1), men and women have reproduced themselves in the miracle of human birth. But after all these centuries, most of us hardly deserve a passing grade in parenting.

Since the beginning of time every culture has formed guidelines for families, including our own wily Western world of the twenty-first century. Our self-absorption, our rush for riches, and the rapid technological changes that isolate individuals and fragment our families at an unprecedented pace demand that parents review and reevaluate basic principles over and over again. Dr. Larry Mercer, outstanding student of American families and able professor of young men and women, employs a keen eye and a skillful hand in crafting a readable and practical tool for mothers and fathers who truly care about producing families of high character.

No document in history qualifies to speak on the subject of how to rear children more than the revelation of God, who creates new life daily. The parenting process, the Bible says, is a complicated custodial job, a lifeguard position with eternal consequences. Paradoxically, the assignment also reverses the role and makes the caretaker a learner as well as protector, mentor, and responsible guardian. To launch a new life into the world and at the same time preserve one's own sanity and usefulness requires a sacrificial nobility and a purposeful strategy unlike any other enterprise.

The dispatch of young lives into our murky environment of indifference and resistance to godly living places parenting in the column of most dangerous occupations. No parent can afford to proceed without adequate protection and know-how. Dr. Mercer's excellent biblical research and conclusions provide such an armor of defense. It is a handbook to be read and reread, discussed, and practiced.

Christian families will always still struggle because we reproduce after our own kind, sinners giving birth to new sinners. Yet God has provided for us "how to" directions for nurturing the next generations. In His plan even failures and detours of disaster can be salvaged. Furthermore, He clearly enunciates the standards for judging the final grade. God puts parenting within the reach of humble, willing hearts. *A Gift from God* arranges these principles in a most applicable fashion; this volume of excellent value belongs on the bedstand—and in the thinking processes—of every parent.

HOWARD G. HENDRICKS
DISTINGUISHED PROFESSOR AND CHAIRMAN
CENTER FOR CHRISTIAN LEADERSHIP
DALLAS THEOLOGICAL SEMINARY

ACKNOWLEDGMENTS

I am grateful for the encouragement of the fine staff at Moody Press. From my initial discussions with the vice president of publishing, Greg Thornton, that gave me the confidence and coaching to get me started, to the editorial support provided by Dr. Anne Scherich and other outstanding support staff, this has been a fun and challenging experience. Thank God for the privilege of working with such an outstanding group of publishing professionals.

I am also grateful for some very dear friends who made themselves available to help with this project. The careful review of the first draft and helpful suggestions by Joann Das, Marilyn Poynter Skemp, and Vornadette Simpson have greatly improved the quality of the final product. Thank God for friends who had the patience and skill to read and comment with sensitivity and support.

In recent years I have had the privilege of testing some of these ideas and convictions in a number of churches and other ministry settings. Oak

Cliff Bible Fellowship, Cornerstone Baptist Church, High Pointe Baptist Church, New Song Bible Fellowship, Northeast Baptist Temple, Cedine Bible Conference and Retreat Center, and Buckener Benevolences have all given me a special forum in recent years to minister to parents. So thanks to Dr. Anthony Evans and Dr. Martin Hawkins of Oak Cliff Bible Fellowship and to Dr. Toby Snowden at High Pointe, Dr. Bernard Fuller at New Song, Dr. Lynwood Davis of Northeast Baptist Temple, Reverend Dwight McKissic at Cornerstone, the staff at Cedine, and Dr. Kenneth Hall at Buckner for entrusting me with a platform to refine in their churches some of the key concepts of this book.

Then to a few other people that have been a special encouragement I owe a special thanks. Thanks to Karen Loritts and Jerry and Elaine Haynes, whose confidence in me led to the persistent question, "Is your book finished yet?" To my dear sister in Christ, H. Johanna Fisher, for her encouragement and for helping give me a forum to share my ideas over the years.

Finally, to my family. It all started with Edward and Helen Mercer, who brought me into the world, and words cannot express the impact my mother's faith has had on this child from North Carolina. Thank God for a wonderful wife and children, who were willing to hear my ideas as this book was being written and who let me tell our personal story as a family to people we may never meet. But most of all they have taught me that God doesn't need perfect people to serve as parents—just people who are willing to be faithful. Every day that Annie and I have the privilege of being their parents we are reminded that our children are gifts from God.

INTRODUCTION

In many ways writing a book is like preaching a sermon. It should affect the preacher just as much as it does the listener. Well, that has certainly been the case for me writing this book. I am on the same journey you are on—looking for directions from God on how to effectively parent. I just have a sense of calling to write this book.

Along the way there are some things I have written and thank God that we have no regrets that the correct biblical principles and approaches were practiced in our home. For more than twenty-one years Annie and I have tried to do our best to honor our children with a home and instruction aimed at helping them achieve God's purpose for their lives. We are thankful for the privilege of giving a lot of positive instruction and nurture over the last twenty-one years.

Then there are principles and insights recorded in this book that, upon reflection, I found myself saying, "I wish we had done that better." So don't be confused. I have not been a perfect parent and have made my share of mistakes. I must admit we started out trying to make "parental perfection" our ambition and passion. Somewhere along the way we realized that although the goal was worthy, it would always be in front of us. We are thankful God's grace is larger than any of our failures as parents.

This incredible journey and search for insight to help my parenting has taught me a great deal, including the fact that there are incredible insights from science that illustrate the relevance and power of the Scripture. I am pleased that this book includes a number of "parenting insights" that may save you much frustration and your child personal pain as he or she grows from childhood to the status of an adult.

You may be asking, Where does the insight for this book come from? Not only have I, as a father, watched my children grow but my personal convictions about parenting have been both challenged and enriched by a number of professional experiences.

- I will never forget some of the lessons I learned walking the halls of a junior high school as a counselor to children on the brink of being removed from their parents' homes.
- Watching men in an adult prison setting as a counselor and sometimes hearing their tragic stories with tears in their eyes convinced me that we need to passionately teach parents how to raise their children compassionately and carefully.
- My experience teaching and counseling parents for a number of years in a local church setting as an associate pastor convinced me that the challenges of parenting are real and the power of the local church is an important part of God's strategy to address the issues of raising children in a world that often rejects Christ.
- As a staff person directly responsible for their care and as an administrator in charge of all facets of a large program, seeing children come into the juvenile system gave me a window into the hearts, minds, and homes of children in crisis that could not have been created by thousands of classroom lessons.
- Serving as administrator and executive director of a large multifaceted Christian social service ministry illustrated the impact compassionate caring adults and innovative ministries can make in the lives of children and families facing challenging life situations.

But none of those experiences would be the answer I would give as to where the ultimate authority for this book comes from. Those experiences are illustrative, not authoritative.

So where does the authority for this book come from? The answer to that question is really simple. It comes from the application of the timeless truths of Scripture to contemporary parenting challenges and opportunities. The Scripture is the only thing that has the element of perfection.

Then there is the insight that comes from successfully, and unsuccessfully, applying the principles of Scripture to the process of raising children. Yes. I have been in both categories during my parenting journey. I can look back with excitement on moments of great success. And as much as I wish I didn't have to admit it, looking back over my shoulder I see some moments that being able to push a delete button and erase would be fun.

But failure doesn't have to be fatal. In some ways I believe the combination of the truths of Scripture, my successful application of Scripture in personal experience as a parent, and lessons learned from personal failure will make this book helpful to you. My goal is to follow my youngest son's advice: "Keep it real." In some ways, I believe that my experience as an imperfect parent will protect you from me making simplistic statements about the processes of parenting that are not relevant to the challenges you face. At least, I hope so.

Let me give you a personal invitation to relax as you read this book. While there may be a number of challenging statements made, your audience is God. He is the One who knows exactly what you need and how to make the Scripture and illustrations fit your personal situation perfectly. That sure takes the pressure off me. So if you approach this book with an open mind and willing heart, God can use it in your life as a parent and enrich the life of your child—*a gift from God.*

1

ON LOAN FROM GOD

Steward of Divine Life

I remember sitting in the doctor's office more than twenty years ago anxiously waiting for Annie or the doctor to come and summon me to the examining room. This had become a familiar routine after more than nine months. This visit was not normal, though, because we knew Annie was very close to delivering our first child.

As I sat, sweaty palms and all, my imagination ran wild. My mind wandered as I waited. *What will happen to this young child that God is entrusting to our care? Are we ready to handle such an awesome responsibility? What will this child become?* As questions like this ran across my mind, I soon heard what I had been waiting for. Her water had broken during the examination. The doctor's instructions were simple. Go home, get your things, and go to the hospital. The long-awaited time had come.

We grabbed our personal belongings and rushed from the doctor's office to wrap up some loose ends at home. Annie's adrenaline was so high that when we got home she cleaned the house, washed a load of dishes, and off to the hospital we went. Our journey into the challenges of parenting was cranking up full throttle. Little did we know we were only in the early stages of one of the most important and enriching journeys of our young lives.

Sitting in that delivery room holding Annie's hand gave me lots of time to think about the wonder of parenting. I reflected on the mystery of the parenting process. It captured my mind and heart. That period of reflection drove me back to the simplicity and truth of God's Word.

EVERY CHILD IS MARKED BY A DIVINE DESIGN

That day God's thoughts in Psalm 139 about the conception and growth of a child suddenly came off the pages of Scripture into a new level of meaning.

> For You formed my inward parts;
> You wove me in my mother's womb.
> I will give thanks to You, for I am fearfully and wonderfully made;
> Wonderful are Your works,
> And my soul knows it very well.
> My frame was not hidden from You,
> When I was made in secret,
> And skillfully wrought in the depths of the earth;
> Your eyes have seen my unformed substance;
> And in Your book were all written
> The days that were ordained for me,
> When as yet there was not one of them.
>
> —Psalm 139:13–16

As I nervously waited in that hospital delivery room, I realized that those verses written hundreds of years earlier described our child struggling to come from the womb of my young wife into the world. Those timeless truths from Scripture uncovered three powerful biblical truths that described my child, who was still waiting to take his place in the world we were preparing for him. I marvel at the fact that these truths describe every child born into the world—including yours.

Facts About Your Child

1. **Your child was known by God intimately even when he was still in the womb.**
2. **Your child's personality was carefully crafted by God intentionally throughout the conception process.**
3. **Your child was commissioned by God with an individual mission for his life.**

FROM A SINGLE CELL TO A UNIQUE INDIVIDUAL

Even from a biological viewpoint, there is something *very* mysterious about it. The sperm meets the egg. Then something amazing begins to happen. The beginning of life occurs.

Each single cell multiplies and God's greatest creation begins to take a very special form. It is important to understand that from a biblical perspective those cells are not just a mass of tissue; the cells form the nucleus of a person created in the image of God. In fact, when I think about what science now tells us, it amazes me that a glimpse into the womb reveals that those cells develop into a unique, total person in a matter of weeks. Every part of your child (eyes, ears, heart, lungs) is distinguishable from a physical perspective. No wonder the Bible exclaims that our children are "fearfully and wonderfully made."

HUMAN CELLS WITH A DIVINE BLUEPRINT

Science makes it clear from research about human development that the process of child development begins in the mother's womb. In the most basic sense, human life begins at conception. Yet when we consider God's perspective, each bundle of cells not only makes up a human being, it has the very life and purpose of God.

I find great insight in Jeremiah's words about God's plan for his life:

> Now the word of the Lord came to me saying,
> "Before I formed you in the womb I knew you,

And before you were born I consecrated you;
I have appointed you a prophet to the nations."
—Jeremiah 1:4–5

God ordered the steps of Jeremiah's life before he was even born.

Therefore, unless God created Jeremiah differently from our children, each one of our children has the incredible potential to express a unique, divine design. Every child is destined to become a social, emotional, physical, intellectual, and spiritual person of infinite worth and value with unlimited human potential to fulfill his or her God-appointed mission. That means your child has a special purpose for his life and has been created with a blueprint for his life drafted by God. Your child is special to God.

EVERY CHILD IS A GIFT FROM GOD TO HIS PARENTS

It is amazing to think that God places in our hands, as parents, a very special person He intentionally created, gave unique gifts to, and commissioned with a special mission for his life as a gift to us. The psalmist said, "Behold, children are a gift of the Lord, the fruit of the womb is a reward. Like arrows in the hand of a warrior, so are the children of one's youth" (Psalm 127:3–4).

This verse from the Psalms counters any notion that parenting is intended to be a burden. No! It is a great blessing. Sometimes, in the midst of the daily grind, that simple truth can make a big difference. Try to keep in mind that your child is a gift when the normal frustrations of the child-rearing process start to bog you down. It can make a huge difference in the emotional development of your child.

I will never forget the day in my office as associate pastor when Angie was almost pushed into the room by her father. His voice was shaking from the anger that also caused him to tremble. "Angie needs to talk with you." He pushed her in the office. As he rushed away, Angie's sobs caused her entire body to heave.

Her opening words caused me pain as her hurt came with her tears. "He said I would never amount to anything. I guess he was right!" Her father's words to her many years earlier had become a self-fulfilling prophecy. In a moment of frustration, Angie's father had told her she would never amount to anything. For the rest of her teenage years, she struggled with self-doubt and feelings of worthlessness. In the midst of his disappointment, Angie's father lost sight of the fact that his daughter was a gift from God.

Yes, when she told me what had caused her father's anger, it was clear that family trust had been violated. But she still was a gift from God. She still deserved to be treated with dignity and respect. As she sat in my office and retraced what led up to this crisis point in her life, it was clear that from her earliest years of childhood she had never lived up to her parents' expectations. As do all parents, her mother and father had a dream for her life. Perhaps they were so focused on their dream they didn't focus on God's plan.

GOD'S PLAN OR YOUR DREAM?

The question is, Will you focus on *God's* plan or *your* dream for your child? A child's birth launches the thoughts that become dreams for us as parents. Parents' dreams start the moment they know a child is to be born into their family and are heightened as they welcome their child into the world. Many dreaming parents see those cells, now a child, becoming an artist, a musician, a builder, an educator, an inventor, a theologian, or one of a myriad other exciting professions.

While dreaming is fun, we have to move to the point in the parenting process where we embrace the challenges and joys of helping our children fulfill *God's* plan for their lives. It is absolutely amazing to consider that God has special works planned for our children to uniquely perform.

You are saying, What makes you say that?

The apostle Paul made that clear when he shared these words with the believers at Ephesus: "For we are His workmanship, created in Christ Jesus for good works, which God prepared beforehand so that we would walk in them" (Ephesians 2:10). The words Paul used to teach the Christians at Ephesus apply to your child. Your child is uniquely equipped to do things for God that no other child on earth can do.

What can you do? You should dream on, but you can't be satisfied with only dreaming.

GUIDING YOUR CHILD TO GOD'S GOAL FOR HIS LIFE

As a dreamer, you must become a Christian parent. That means God wants you to become a steward of the cells that became your child. God wants you to enjoy a relationship with your child. Every Christian parent must see the potential. But the parent who wants to please God must also accept the responsibility and anticipate the problems. As a committed parent you can expect happiness, but the process will also present opportunities to endure hardship.

You must be willing to submit your efforts to God and pray that your dreams fit in with God's plan. You must ask God to let you have a glimpse of His plan for the life of your child. Then you can start dreaming and working to make that dream a reality. Proverbs says: "Train up a child in the way he should go, even when he is old he will not depart from it" (Proverbs 22:6).

What a challenge! What a privilege—guiding your child to achieving God's goals for his life! That is not something we can do in our own strength. It takes a parent who submits his parental actions to God and makes God's plan more important than his preferences.

YOU WON'T BE PERFECT

By now you may be starting to feel tightness in your chest because the responsibilities of parenting seem so great. Let me warn you. Don't think that you can be a perfect parent. The perfect parent does not exist. And even if from a human viewpoint someone achieved the status of perfection as a parent, that would not guarantee he would have perfect children.

God, of course, was and is a perfect parent to His children. He created Adam and Eve. God gave His first children a perfect environment and perfect access to Himself. Adam and Eve had everything they needed for physical, spiritual, and emotional security. Yet they still chose to disobey God. God's perfection did not dictate that His children display complete obedience. Every child has the freedom to choose whether he will obey his parents or follow the pull of the sin nature we all possess.

YOUR CHILD WON'T BE PERFECT

No matter how good you are as a parent, your child will make poor choices and sometimes break your heart and the heart of God. Like you, he will sin. Why is that so? Well, the words of John in his first epistle forever dispels the notion of the perfect or sinless person, and therefore the perfect child:

> If we say that we have no sin, we are deceiving ourselves and the truth is not in us. If we confess our sins, He is faithful and righteous to forgive us our sins and to cleanse us from all unrighteousness. If we say that we have not sinned, we make Him a liar and His word is not in us. (1 John 1:8–10)

It is important that you don't allow yourself to fall into the trap of thinking that your child will be perfect. We parents need to accept the reality that our children will be, like us, imperfect. One of the key questions is how we model and teach our children to handle human imperfections.

BE FAITHFUL

With this in mind, what is the mark of a biblical parent? The mark of a Christian parent is not perfection, but faithfulness. After over twenty years of ministry experience, I have concluded that a few key practices emerge from the Scripture as foundational practices for Christian parenting. Those practices won't guarantee perfect parents—or perfect children—but they will give our children the foundation they need to achieve God's purpose for their lives.

Paul's affirmation of the childhood experience of Timothy illustrates the kind of parental activity that can give our children a foundation of parental faithfulness. "You, however, continue in the things you have learned and become convinced of, knowing from whom you have learned them, and that from childhood you have known the sacred writings which are able to give you the wisdom that leads to salvation through faith which is in Christ Jesus" (2 Timothy 3:14–15).

At the end of the chapter are some concrete suggestions to help you lay the foundation for leading your child to salvation and the pathway for achieving God's purpose. It may take the rest of your parental lives to really get to where you want to be in the following areas. But these are areas worth your consistent attention and practice.

As we go through the rest of the book, I will give you practical steps for carrying out each of these seven foundational principles. You won't be able to put all of these steps into practice overnight. In fact, you will never reach the point where you do any of them perfectly (remember, there's no such thing as a perfect parent). But you can be faithful.

At a certain stage in my life as a parent, I reached a point of personal freedom when I realized that my parenting would not be perfect. Like you, I am on a journey to stand before God at the end of my parenting journey and hear Him say, "You were faithful." That is my passion and my focus. Along the way, my dream is that Annie's and my children would reach God's destination for their lives.

One of the joys of writing this book is to have the privilege of sharing truths about parenting from Scripture and more than twenty years of personal and ministry experience. But, for now, start where you are. It will be both challenging and rewarding. You will experience frustrations and joys. When you think about the challenge, remember the words of Mamie Gene Cole:

THE CHILD'S APPEAL

I am the Child.
All the world waits for my coming.
All the earth watches with interest to see what I will become
Civilization hangs in the balance
For what I am, the world of tomorrow will be.

I am the Child.
I have come into your world, about which I know nothing.
Why I came I know not;
How I came I know not.
I am curious; I am interested.

I am the Child.
You hold in your hand my destiny.
You determine, largely, whether I shall succeed or fail.
Give me, I pray you, those things that make for happiness.
Train me, I beg you, that I may be a blessing to the world.[1]

FAITH STEPS

Foundational Practices

1. Pray for your child every day.

2. Communicate spiritual truth to your child every day.

3. Encourage your child every day.

4. Provide for your child's unique needs every day.

5. Protect your child every day.

6. Model personal holiness for your child every day.

7. Promote responsibility in the life of your child every day.

A PARENT'S PRAYER

Father, Thank You for the gift You gave me through the life of my child. Help me continually to see the uniqueness of my child and my part in the blueprint for his life. I am excited about the fact that life has a special plan and purpose. My dream is that I fulfill my responsibilities to help shape his character and support him as he makes important life decisions. Free me from the quicksand of perfectionistic thoughts that will stifle the emotional life of my child and short-circuit his ability to experience a lifetime of joy. But please, Lord, help me to be faithful on a daily basis to disciple him in accordance with Your Word and by the power of the Holy Spirit. Amen.

PARENTING INSIGHTS

SPECIAL CARE INSTRUCTIONS

Research Highlight: Your Child's Prenatal Development

Your child's development in the womb is fascinating. Here are a few facts to help you understand the importance of prenatal care and development. Joan Raymond shares some powerful insights in a *Newsweek* Special Issue.

> *A baby's journey through the realm of the senses begins in the womb. By the seventh month, nerves connecting the eyes and the brain's visual cortex have begun to function in a rudimentary way. . . . Nerves that relay touch perception appear on the skin of the fetus by about the 10th week. . . . By the fourth month, the somatosensory cortex—the part of the brain that registers tactile perception—is coming online. . . . By about 28 weeks, the fetus will respond to loud noises. Taste buds make an appearance at a remarkably early seven weeks. . . . And although the fetus doesn't smell in the conventional sense, it can absorb odors in the amniotic fluid by the 24th week of gestation.*[2]

We also know that "the food a child consumes—in the womb, during infancy and as a toddler—can have lasting effects on her habits and her health," Stephen P. Williams reports in *Newsweek*. That's why God has built the human body to work hard to protect your child in the womb. "During pregnancy" Williams says, "some of the most nutritious foods in a woman's diet may suddenly turn her stomach. . . . Most plants in the human diet, especially those with strong or bitter tastes, contain natural pesticides. While these toxins are not usually strong enough to harm children or adults, some may pose hazards to developing embryos. In her 1995 book, *Pregnancy Sickness: Using Your Body's Natural Defenses to Protect Your Baby-to-Be*, evolutionist Margie Profet showed that 'morning sickness,' which lasts from the third week into the second trimester, coincides with the formation of limbs, organs, and the nervous system.

Moreover, it causes aversion to the very foods—foods like cabbage, Brussels sprouts, garlic, basil, mushrooms, nutmeg and fish—that are most likely to disrupt development."[3]

RESEARCH APPLICATIONS

Here are the things you should do to support your child's prenatal development.

- Take folic acid daily prior to and after the termination of your pregnancy.
- Eat plenty of fruits and vegetables.
- Screen as many unwholesome things off your diet as possible.
- Avoid foods that your stomach rejects while you are pregnant.
- Make sure you take care of your physical and emotional health as a gift to your child.

"For You formed my inward parts; You wove me in my mother's womb" (Psalm 139:13).

Ask God to give you a way to help you give your child the best prenatal care possible.

2

BY DIVINE DESIGN

Discover and Encourage Your Child's Uniqueness

"Venus in own orbit."

This January 2001 *Chicago Tribune* headline described the $40 million dollar endorsement deal signed by tennis star Venus Williams. Later in the article the writer made this comment.

> There has never been a female equivalent, as a performer or as a product endorser. With her personality, skill, worldwide recognition, and tendency to be a bit controversial . . . "You have players who are as good as Venus, but they don't have the personality or the total package," said Keith Davis, the attorney who negotiated the Reebok contract for Williams.[1]

While she is an outstanding tennis player, Venus is also unique. But so is your child, even though she may never sign a $40 million endorsement deal.

RECOGNIZE THAT YOUR CHILD IS UNIQUE

Your child is uniquely created by God and has a purpose that only she can fulfill. Isn't that amazing to think about? You have the incredible privilege of being a steward of the life of a person sent on a mission by God. Paul captured that thought in his letter to the church at Ephesus: "For we are His workmanship, created in Christ Jesus for good works, which God prepared beforehand so that we would walk in them" (Ephesians 2:10). That verse describes every individual. It includes you and your child as well. Don't move past that spiritual and practical reality too quickly.

As you wake up every day and look at, listen to, and talk with your child, never forget that she is special. Remembering that will help you get through the mundane activities of life with a little more zeal and sense of purpose. Try to not lose the wonder of that fact.

CELEBRATE YOUR CHILD'S UNIQUENESS

If you don't lose the wonder, it will help you find a spirit of celebration more than consternation during the joys and challenges of your daily responsibilities. I love the way the psalmist celebrates his uniqueness in a way that all of us can learn from as parents.

> For You formed my inward parts; . . .
> I will give thanks to You, for I am fearfully and wonderfully made;
> Wonderful are Your works,
> And my soul knows it very well.
> My frame was not hidden from You,
> When I was made in secret,
> And skillfully wrought in the depths of the earth;
> Your eyes have seen my unformed substances;
> And in Your book were all written
> The days that were ordained for me,
> When as yet there was not one of them.
>
> —Psalm 139:13–16

Remember how you treat fine china or special jewelry? You handle these objects with a spirit of care and precision. Even on your worst days, you probably have not thrown your china across the room or carelessly handled an expensive watch. Your child is far more important and special than any piece of fine china or jewelry you will ever own or see in your lifetime. Celebrate that reality.

Tell your child how unique and special she is. Share your recognition of the uniqueness of your child with other people.

Your continual acknowledgement of this reality will make some very important deposits into your child's bank and serve her well for years to come. Make sure your child knows that even if no one else recognizes her uniqueness, you do.

DON'T LET YOUR CHILD BE STIFLED BY SOCIAL AND PHYSICAL CHALLENGES

Social and physical circumstances don't have to determine your child's potential. One of the things you can do is to give your child a spirit that helps her recognize that God's plan does not have to take a backseat to anything if she is willing to give of herself and trust God completely.

The book of Exodus makes it clear that God had a special plan for the life of Moses in spite of the fact he was born in difficult social circumstances and with physical limitations. When Moses tried to use his circumstances and disabilities as an excuse for not pursuing God's plan, God's response was instructive to Moses and illustrative to all of us as parents.

> Then Moses said to the Lord, "Please Lord, I have never been eloquent, neither recently nor in time past, nor since You have spoken to Your servant; for I am slow of speech and slow of tongue." The Lord said to him, "Who has made man's mouth? Or who makes him mute or deaf, or seeing or blind? Is it not I, the Lord? Now then go, and I, even I, will be with your mouth, and teach you what you are to say." (Exodus 4:10–12)

Any limitation Moses had did not limit God's ability to use Moses to glorify Him. The same thing is true for your child, or any other child.

HELP YOUR CHILD RECOGNIZE HER GIFTS AND ABILITIES

Do not allow your child to lose sight of her uniqueness as she interacts with her peers and other people in her world. There will be many challenges. Some will want your child to see herself through the eyes of others rather than the eyes of God. Don't let that happen. The most important measure of your child's significance is what God thinks about her.

Part of your opportunity as a parent is to hold back the onslaught of people who will repeatedly want your child to give up her individuality to become just another number in the crowd. You can do that most powerfully by reminding her every day through the words of your lips and the example of your life that she is unique.

"DECLONE" YOUR CHILD

Here is where you have a special challenge. Your child will be tempted to be satisfied to look, sound, and act like her peers. Many of your child's peers will simply be satisfied to operate with a "Clone Mentality."

You have the opportunity to help your child identify with her peers without assimilating inappropriate patterns of behavior. Practically speaking, that means you have to carefully evaluate and examine her clothing and the other paraphernalia of growing up to make sure it does not encourage a negative level of assimilation with her peers. God does not make copies. In the Old Testament book of Daniel, we see that he understood the power of pursuing personal conviction rather than simply following the crowd and the prevailing view of everyone else in the culture. The passage below chronicles Daniel's experience with his peers and his culture. He stood by his conviction against both, and God honored his faithfulness.

> Then the king ordered Ashpenaz, the chief of his officials, to bring in some of the sons of Israel, including some of the royal family and of the nobles, youths in whom was no defect, who were good-looking, showing intelligence in every branch of wisdom, endowed with understanding and discerning knowledge, and who had ability for serving in the king's court; and he ordered him to teach them the literature and language of the Chaldeans. The

> king appointed for them a daily ration from the king's choice food and from the wine which he drank, and appointed that they should be educated three years, at the end of which they were to enter the king's personal service. Now among them from the sons of Judah were Daniel, Hananiah, Mishael and Azariah. Then the commander of the officials assigned new names to them; and to Daniel he assigned the new name Belteshazzar, to Hannaiah Shadrach, to Mishael Meshach, and Azariah Abed-nego.
>
> But Daniel made up his mind that he would not defile himself with the king's choice food or with the wine which he drank; so he sought permission from the commander of the officials that he might not defile himself. (Daniel 1:3–8)

Daniel demonstrated incredible willingness to go against social and political pressure to follow God's conviction for his life. Sometimes God will place your child in a difficult situation to accomplish His purpose.

Your child needs to know that in spite of those circumstances, God has called her to be faithful to His purpose for her life. The prophet Daniel's life offers a solid example of the importance of staying focused on God's purpose rather than what is popular and convenient. We can learn about the kinds of things we need to teach our children about the importance of staying true to God.

Every child God makes is an original. I am always awed by the thought that there are no identical fingerprints, grains of sand, or snowflakes. And certainly every child is made with an original blueprint by God as a trophy of His creative majesty. Since that is true, "declone" your child by helping her live up to her created purpose. Does that mean your child doesn't need acceptance from other people? No. Your child does need this acceptance. What she doesn't need is acceptance through illegitimate avenues.

CREATE LEGITIMATE AVENUES OF SUCCESS

I have always believed a child who feels she doesn't have a legitimate avenue of success will create an illegitimate one. Unfortunately, many times drug use, negative peer selections, and other forms of self-destructive behavior come as a child seeks to find some way of expressing the potential locked up within her.

Help your child let this potential out by creating legitimate avenues of success. Be a student of your children's interests, talents, and abilities. Then do everything you can to help her pursue interests that will allow her to experience personal success.

The potential avenues of success can be far-reaching and include options like music, art, theatre, sports, and agriculture. Keep looking until you find something that captures your child's imagination and interest. Then cultivate it. It won't easy.

FOSTER YOUR CHILD'S RESPECT FOR THE INDIVIDUAL STRENGTHS OF OTHERS

Your child needs to lean on other people's strengths, just like you do. Don't ever let her forget that she cannot achieve God's purpose for her life without other people. A wonderful story in William Bennet's *Book of Virtues* illustrates this truth in a powerful way.

THE REBELLION AGAINST THE STOMACH

Once a man had a dream in which his hands and feet and mouth and brain all began to rebel against his stomach. "You good-for-nothing sluggard!" the hands said. "We work all day long, sawing and hammering and lifting and carrying. By evening we're covered with blisters and scratches, and our joints ache, and we're covered with dirt. And meanwhile you just sit there, hogging all the food."

"We agree!" cried the feet. "Think how sore we get, walking back and forth all day long. And you just stuff yourself full, you greedy pig, so that you're that much heavier to carry about."

"That's right!" whined the mouth. "Where do you think all that food you love comes from? I'm the one who has to chew it all up, and as soon as I'm finished you suck it all down for yourself. Do you call that fair?"

"And what about me?" called the brain. "Do you think it's easy being up here, having to think about where your next meal is going to come from? And yet I get nothing at all for my pains."

And one by one the parts of the body joined the complaint against the stomach, which didn't say anything at all.

"I have an idea," the brain finally announced. "Let's all rebel against this lazy belly, and stop working for it."

"Superb idea!" all the other members and organs agreed. "We'll teach you how important we are, you pig. Then maybe you'll do a little work of your own."

So they all stopped working. The hands refused to do any lifting or carrying. The feet refused to walk. The mouth promised not to chew or swallow a single bite. And the brain swore it wouldn't come up with any more bright ideas. At first the stomach growled a bit, as it always did when it was hungry. But after a while it was quiet.

Then, to the dreaming man's surprise, he found he could not walk. He could not grasp anything in his hands. He could not even open his mouth. And he suddenly began to feel rather ill.

The dream seemed to go on for several days. As each day passed, the man felt worse and worse. "This rebellion had better not last much longer," he thought to himself, "or I'll starve."

Meanwhile, the hands and feet and mouth and brain just lay there, getting weaker and weaker. At first they roused themselves just enough to taunt the stomach every once in a while, but before long they didn't even have the energy for that.

Finally the man heard a faint voice coming from the direction of his feet.

"It could be that we were wrong," they were saying. "We suppose the stomach might have been working in his own way all along."

"I was just thinking the same thing," murmured the brain. "It's true he's been getting all the food. But it seems he's been sending most of it right back to us."

"We might as well admit our error," the mouth said. "The stomach has just as much work to do as the hands and feet and brain and teeth."

"Then let's all get back to work," they cried together. And at that the man woke up.

To his relief, he discovered his feet could walk again. His hands could grasp, his mouth could chew, and his brain could now think clearly. He began to feel much better.

"Well, there's a lesson for me," he thought as he filled his stomach at breakfast. "Either we all work together, or nothing works at all."[2]

It is a careful tightrope balancing respect and reflecting their uniqueness, but with your help your child can learn to walk it. Help your child develop healthy respect for her peers without letting her personal identity be determined by the values of others. That means she needs to experience personal success that is not dependent on peers only.

TEACH YOUR CHILD THAT CHILDREN WITH CHALLENGES ARE SPECIAL IN GOD'S SIGHT TOO

Another important element of respect your child needs to develop is respect for people who are different physically and emotionally. You can give your child a great gift if you help her recognize that all children are created in the image of God, even those who have special needs.

This is especially important now that schools are trying hard to make sure that children with disabilities are included in the regular classroom experience as much as possible. In fact, a recent survey indicated that during the 1996–97 school year 46 percent of the 6 million students with disabilities in the United States spent at least 80 percent of their school day in regular classrooms.[3]

There are a number of kinds of disabilities your child could be exposed to in either a school or community setting. These disabilities are identified in the (IDEA) Individuals with Disabilities Education Act and refer to the official group recognized as factors that negatively impact a child's ability to learn.

Attention deficit/hyperactivity disorder: A pattern of inattention and/or hyperactivity-impulsivity.

Autism: A developmental disability significantly affecting verbal and nonverbal communication and social interaction.

Blindness and low vision

Communication disorders: Either a speech or a language disorder.

Emotional or behavioral disorders: One or more of five characteristics, including inappropriate behavior and inability to build relationships.

Giftedness: Children who give evidence of high-performance capability.

Hearing loss: IDEA divides this category into "deafness" and "hearing impairments."

Learning disabilities: A disorder in the "basic psychological processes" involved in understanding or in using language, spoken or written.
Mental retardation: Substantial limitations in functioning.
Multiple and severe disabilities: "Multiple" means concomitant impairments; "severe" refers to children who, because of the intensity of their physical, mental, or emotional problems, need highly specialized services.
Other health impairments: Due to chronic or acute health problems, these kids have limited strength, vitality, or alertness.
Physical disabilities: A severe orthopedic impairment.
Traumatic brain injury: An acquired injury to the brain caused by an external physical force.[4]

If a child in your family has special challenges or disabilities, remind her that she is of infinite worth and value to God, just like any other child. The challenges she faces do not diminish her worth to God and should not impact how she interacts with another child who has special needs. That simply means that your child has more opportunity to demonstrate the love of Christ to another child with special challenges.

Jesus presents a compelling model of compassion for all of us to follow. He had special compassion for those who had physical and emotional challenges. Just a cursory examination of the Gospels reveals a God with great compassion for those with special challenges. If Jesus had that kind of compassion, we should seek to develop sensitivity and compassion in the hearts of our children for those who are experiencing special difficulties in their lives.

Begin at your child's earliest age to let her see other children through the heart of God. Here's where your personal example is powerful. Treat people who have special physical and emotional challenges with respect and dignity. That will do more to help your child in this area than your words ever could.

So how do you respond spiritually and practically?

LET GOD'S GLORY OVERSHADOW PHYSICAL DIFFICULTIES AND/OR LIMITATIONS

Sometimes your child will have to overcome tremendous personal obstacles to experience her full potential, or will come into contact with a child in this situation. Although it is difficult to understand, God's glory can sometimes be illustrated in a very special way as you and your child learn to focus on God's glory of personal strength. I can only point you for encouragement to the Scriptures and to the example of a person I believe is a modern example of almost saintly strength.

A classic passage of Scripture suggests that sometimes God chooses to allow limitations in a child's life, even from birth, to bring Him special glory.

> As He passed by, He saw a man blind from birth. And His disciples asked Him, "Rabbi, who sinned, this man or his parents, that he would be born blind?" Jesus answered, " It was neither that this man sinned, nor his parents; but it was so that the works of God might be displayed in him." (John 9:1–3)

Simply stated, when a child has special needs, it is not our task to judge or even to understand the answers to all the "Why?" questions. Our privilege is to love such a child unconditionally with the love of Christ and give her the opportunity to achieve God's full purpose for her life.

TEACH YOUR CHILD THAT THERE ARE NO ACCIDENTS WITH GOD

I love the words of Fanny Crosby as she looked back on God's sovereign work in and through her life. Her perspective should be the conviction of every person born into this world.

In her autobiography Fanny Crosby comments on the doctor who unwittingly caused her blindness:

> I have heard that this physician never ceased expressing his regret at the occurrence; and that it was one of the sorrows of his life. But if I could meet him now, I would say, "Thank you, thank you, over and over again for making me blind." Although it may have been a blunder on the physician's part, it was no mistake on God's. I verily believe it was His intention that I should live my days in physical darkness, so as to be better prepared to sing His praises and incite others to do so.

Thus by a doctor's apparent mistake, God gave to the church the wonderful heritage of a blind Fanny Crosby who, with her increased spiritual insight, was able to write thousands of enduring hymns.

FAITH STEPS

1. Explain to your child that she is uniquely created.
2. Help your child discover her uniqueness.
3. Involve your child in regular activities to cultivate her interests and talents.
4. Give your child special support in areas where it is recognized that she has limitations.
5. Expose your child to positive Christian mentors and role models who excel in her area of interest.

A PARENT'S PRAYER

Father, Thank You that my child is unique. Help me guide her through the process of recognizing and fully using the special talents and abilities You have given her. Give my child the energy and passion to see past any of her personal limitations and grasp the wonderful potential she has in You. Lead us to and keep us in that place where we are in the center of Your will. Amen.

PARENTING INSIGHTS

SPECIAL CARE INSTRUCTIONS

Research Highlight: Your Child's Brain

There is an explosive body of literature that reveals new information about the development of a child's brain that could have profound impact on your parenting practices.

RESEARCH HIGHLIGHTS

- The growth and development of the brain begins in the womb of the mother with the following milestones:
  4 months of gestation—process tactile sensations
  7 months of gestation—rudimentary visual signals can be processed
  28 weeks of gestation—auditory cortex (hearing) can perceive loud noises
- The type of food a child consumes can severely impact her level of brain functioning.
- Your child's experiences will change her brain physiologically, and her environment will have a determining influence on its ultimate level of functioning.
- Your child's capacity to absorb and assimilate information (IQ) is not determined at birth.
- Your child's brain growth and development will be greatly impacted by her emotions.
- The level of functioning of your child's brain will impact every other realm of her experience.
- Children, teenagers, and adults have very different levels of capacity in brain functioning.
- No two brains are alike.[5]

These research results give a strong motivation for some careful actions on the part of parents early in a child's life to help her develop to her full brain-functioning potential.

RESEARCH APPLICATIONS

1. Every mother should make sure she takes care of her body by eating a healthy and nutritious diet daily while pregnant for the sake of the baby's health.
2. Every mother should prepare healthy, nutritious meals for her child so that she can maximize the growth potential of the child.
3. Create a positive and stimulating environment for the child at home and away from the home.
4. Use music to promote the growth and development of your child's brain.
5. Set realistic behavioral and emotional goals based on your child's brain capacity to function.
6. Minimize the stresses in your child's life that may minimize her brain functioning.
7. Resist the temptation to inappropriately compare the brain functioning of your child with other children.

"Your eyes have seen my unformed substance; and in Your book were all written the days that were ordained for me, when as yet there was not one of them" (Psalm 139:16).

Maximize your child's brain functioning by making sure she has the best possible nutrition and experiences to promote her growth and development.

3

FRAGILE: HANDLE WITH CARE

Nurturing Your Child's Emotional Temperament

Sometimes God uses simple experiences to teach us profound spiritual truth. Let me tell you about one such experience in the life of our family.

When my oldest child was only three years old, he had an accident and did not quite make it to the bathroom. From the odor that enveloped the room, it soon became quite apparent to Annie and me what had happened.

The scene turned into a mixture of humor and a classic illustration I have never forgotten of how easy it is for a parent to provoke his child to incorrect behavior.

It's confession time.

I walked into the room and asked my son, "What happened?" He did not quite know whether to confess his accident or not. His first response was, "I don't know."

I thought, *That's the wrong answer.* So I asked the question again. "What happened?" It was apparent that he was becoming more uncomfortable. He really didn't give me an answer. But my investigation continued as we both stood in the room.

When I asked the question the third time, his response taught me a lesson that has stayed with me for more than *twenty* years. By then he seemed pretty flustered, and he blurted out, "Daniel did it!" Daniel was his best friend at the time. He lived on the other side of town, and as far as we knew he was at home enjoying time with his family.

As we gently corrected him and cleaned him up, I knew my approach needed to change. Later, Annie and I privately chuckled, but we—well, it was I—learned a lesson that day about provoking a child to error. My question had prompted my three-year-old child to misrepresent what had happened. (Give me a break. I was a young father.)

That incident early in the life of our children reinforces for me even now the value of sensitivity with children. It helps me understand Paul's words in Ephesians 6:4: "Fathers, do not provoke your children to anger, but bring them up in the discipline and instruction of the Lord."

DON'T AGITATE YOUR CHILD SO THAT HE LOSES HEART

That verse shows the positive and the negative side of the nurturing process. Parents—and fathers, specifically—are challenged not just to say the right things to their children but also to avoid saying or doing things that would agitate their children to become angry. Wow!

God is concerned about your child's emotional and spiritual life. If you want to honor God as you parent your children, that means your sensitivity to words and actions that agitate your children is important to God. The teaching of Proverbs 15:1 will be instructive for you: "A gentle answer turns away wrath, but a harsh word stirs up anger."

What a powerful insight to reflect upon. Harsh words and actions can provoke anger in our children. Your response may have not only a great impact on your child's level of anger in your home but can also help shape his response to difficult situations. Consciously work to avoid agitating your child to anger.

REMEMBER THAT A CHILD'S HEART IS VERY SENSITIVE

That warning in Ephesians stretches the thinking of all parents and gives us motivation to consider similar instructions God gives parents in a parallel section of Scripture. God places a strong emphasis on the emotional state of children. He wants parents to help their children maintain emotional stability. Colossians 3:21 says, "Fathers, do not exasperate your children, so that they will not lose heart." This passage moves beyond anger and focuses on the importance of not causing a child to lose heart.

Annie related an interesting experience she had when one of my daughters was in the first grade. My daughter's teacher had given all the students a little plastic cup with a teabag on the inside. These words were on the outside of the cup:

Here is a gift for Mothers' Day
I will try my best in every way.
But when you get upset with me,
Relax and have a cup of tea.

My daughter had displayed such a sweet disposition that my wife felt she would never have a reason to get mad at her. She was trying to affirm my daughter and said, "Well, I guess I will never use that cup of tea." When my daughter heard her mother say that, she broke into tears because she thought my wife was rejecting her.

Obviously, that was a misunderstanding, but it shows how sensitive a child's heart can be. The heart is so important that God's Word challenges all of us to keep our hearts open and pure. There is a simple admonition in Proverbs 4:23: "Watch over your heart with all diligence, for from it flow the springs of life."

As a parent, you have to guard the heart of your child. That could begin with a commitment to help him see himself as God sees him. That is why it is so important to help your child see what God's Word says about his worth and value.

Here are some keys that may help you build biblical self-esteem in the heart of your child.

Keys to Building Biblical Self-esteem in Your Child

1. **Help him understand God's love for him by recognizing God's goodness.**
2. **Express your love for him on a daily basis.**
3. **Affirm a specific personal quality he possesses as often as you can.**
4. **Give him a smile at every opportunity.**
5. **Allow him to recognize your limitations so that he realizes that nobody is perfect.**
6. **Encourage him to enjoy the gift of laughter.**
7. **Express joy with him in times of celebration and crisis.**

AVOID THE "SIX SINS" IN YOUR DAILY RELATIONSHIPS

You have to make sure you handle with care the daily contacts you have with your child. A good starting point is to avoid what I call "The Six Sins of Parenting." These "Six Sins" are sometimes reflected in statements that could be perceived as ideas that a parent doesn't intend to project.

THE SIX SINS OF PARENTING

1. **"Your brother or sister"**—The parental sin of *comparison* often stifles the emotional security of a child. Your child is an individual. Treat him like one. Don't compare him with his siblings in terms of value or behavior. That will not only hurt the child but damage family relationships.
2. **"You always/never"**—The parental sin of *overstatement* discourages a child and could cause him to lose the motivation to change. Resist the tendency to let your emotions result in words that exaggerate in an unhealthy way for your child.
3. **"Shut up"**—If we are not careful, our words will cause us to commit the parental sin of *dehumanizing our child.* We shut the doors

of trucks and cars. But we can't "shut up" kids. I guess this is a call to us to keep our emotions in check.

4. **"I don't care"**—"Your emotions don't matter to me" is the message the words "I don't care" could send to a child in a moment of conflict between parent and child. This sin of *devaluing a child* could cause him to be attracted to people who act like they care for him but don't really have his best interests in mind.
5. **"I don't have time for you"**—This statement says, "What you want to do is not important enough for me to ever invest my time in it." Obviously, there are times when a parent cannot do things a child would like for him to do. The way we communicate our lack of availability is very important. We want to avoid committing the sin of a *consistent lack of availability* and making a child think we are not interested in things that are important to him. If this message is communicated consistently, a child will feel as though he has little significance to his parent.
6. **"You are stupid"**—You diminish your child's sense of worth when you commit the sin of *assaulting his intellectual capacity.* That's what happens when phrases like this are used by parents in moments of frustration. When you are upset about something your child has done, make a conscious commitment to focus comments on his performance, not his person.

LIBERALLY PRACTICE "THE SEVEN SECRETS OF PARENTING"

Gentleness and sensitivity in the way we respond to our children will prevent damaging comments when we are frustrated with their attitudes and behavior. Certainly, there are negatives we want to avoid doing or saying, but there are also positive things we can do as parents to help develop the emotional stability of our children.

There are some statements you can incorporate into your regular routine that will make your child really feel like he is special. I call these "The Seven Secrets of Parenting." Again, these phrases represent messages and ideas that children need to feel and hear.

THE SEVEN SECRETS OF PARENTING

1. **"Thank you"**—Saying "Thank you" lets your child know you do not take him or the things he does for granted. All of us, even our children, like to hear words of appreciation. That is why the secret of *appreciation* is so important. If you regularly convey an attitude of appreciation, your children will enjoy doing things for you.
2. **"I am sorry"**—Saying "I am sorry" helps communicate that you recognize that your child is experiencing some type of pain. The secret of *emotional connection* creates a strong bond between parent and child. Children, like adults, need to know their parents care when they are hurting.
3. **"I really want to, but can't right now"**—When your time commitments prevent you from being involved with something that is important to your child, it is important you let him know that you want to spend time with him doing things that are important to him. You can use the secret of a *delayed satisfying experience.* Say phrases like, "I can't do it today, but tomorrow I am looking forward to being with you," or, "I am sorry to miss this time, but next time I will certainly be there." Seek to let your child know that the things that matter to him are important to you.
4. **"Help me understand"**—When your child's behavior or words are unclear, you have at least two choices. One is to reject his words or behavior and make him feel insecure. Making your child feel insecure will not strengthen your relationship with him. Another choice you have when you don't understand your child's behavior or actions is to use the secret of *searching for meaning.* Don't be satisfied to stop the communication process with your child when you don't understand his words or actions. Ask him to help you understand what he means. Even if it takes a while for this to happen, he will appreciate your efforts.
5. **"You are special"**—When you let your child know he is special, it helps him deal with any feelings of failure or rejection that may surface in his life. All of us are in a constant search to find some level of significance. That is why giving our children, through our actions, the sense that we value their uniqueness as individuals means that we will employ the secret of *personal recognition.* Knowing we

value them personally will help them handle rejection by peers, failure in school, and other challenges in their lives. Tell them frequently that they are special.

6. **"Please"**—Using this word is not intended to be pleading or begging, but rather to acknowledge that you don't take your child for granted. Especially as they grow older, children are encouraged when their parents use the secret of *dignity* in their interpersonal communication. When you use the word "Please" on a regular basis, your children will appreciate the regard for them that that communicates.
7. **"I love you"**—The Bible's statement that "love covers a multitude of sins" (1 Peter 4:8) is a powerful reminder that love builds bridges in relationships. Saying "I love you" to a child not only builds bridges in your relationship with him but helps to cover any past omissions and breakdowns in your communication and relationship. Communicating your love regularly to your child brings the secret of value into your parenting style and strengthens your child's feelings of self-worth and personal importance.

You may not be able to perfectly use these "Seven Secrets of Parenting," but if you consciously attempt to build emotional security into the life of the child God gave you, He will use your efforts in a very positive way. See your child as a gift with a fragile temperament that, like fine china or a precious jewel, requires gentle and sensitive treatment.

HELP YOUR CHILD RESPOND TO EMOTIONAL TRAUMA

No matter what you do, some type of emotional trauma will find its way into the life of your child. Learn to recognize the causes and characteristics of emotional trauma so that you can help him through difficult periods. The Scripture gives some excellent examples of causes and characteristics of emotional trauma that have a direct impact not only on adults but also on children.

BIBLICAL EXAMPLES OF IMPACT OF EMOTIONAL TRAUMA

Passage	Cause	Characteristic
1 Kings 19:1–8	Persecution, ridicule, failure	Retreat from people
2 Samuel 12:16–23	Death of a loved one	Lack of appetite
Psalm 32	Unconfessed personal sin	Physical deterioration
Psalm 73	Lack of sense of fairness	Desire to quit
Proverbs 13:12	Loss of hope	Sick heart
Matthew 26:36–46	Rejection, socially and spiritually	Tears and distress
2 Corinthians 12:7–10	Physical problems	Sense of urgency

Persecution, ridicule, and failure

If your child has repeated experiences of persecution, ridicule, and failure, it can cause a great deal of emotional trauma that may result in despair and discouragement. The child's natural tendency will be to retreat from you and other people. Be sensitive, so that when and if this happens you are ready to provide the encouragement your child needs.

Death of a loved one

If your child loses someone very important to him, it can cause him a great deal of pain and emotional confusion. Along with other emotional symptoms, one of the results could be a loss of appetite that could symbolize a lack of desire to care for his own health and well-being. You have to make sure that your child's discouragement does not lead to self-destructive behavior.

Unconfessed personal sin

Help your child keep short accounts with God. Unconfessed sin can clog up a child's emotional arteries. Teach your child the importance of admitting his failures to you and to God.

Lack of a sense of fairness

If a child feels like he is not being treated fairly, it will result in emotional pain and discouragement. It is inevitable that your child will experience some unfair treatment. Try to minimize it and equip him to deal with it when it comes.

Rejection, socially and spiritually

One of the greatest needs every person has, including your child, is the need for acceptance. If your child feels rejected a lot, he could face a great deal of tears and distress. That is why your household should be a place of acceptance, no matter how your child is treated outside the home.

Physical problems

Debilitating physical problems impact people physically and emotionally. Address physical problems whenever you can.

BE A BUILDER

This anonymous poem, first shared with me by my longtime friend Andy Hickman, captures the spirit that will be required to handle your child's temperament with the kind of care and sensitivity that honors God and helps your child develop emotional security. You need to build your child's emotional strength through your daily words and actions.

BUILDERS AND WRECKERS

I watched them tearing a building down,
A gang of men in a busy town.

With a Ho-heave-ho and a lusty yell,
They swung a beam and a side wall fell.

I asked the foreman, "Are these men skilled?
The kind you would hire if you had to build?"

He gave a laugh, "No indeed,
Just common labor is all I need."

"For I can easily wreck in a day or two,
What it has taken builders years to do."

And I thought to myself as I went away,
Which of these roles have I had to play.

Am I a builder who works with care,
measuring life by the rule and square?

Shaping my deeds to a well-made plan,
carefully doing the best I can.

Or am I a wrecker walking the town,
content with the labor of tearing down?

FAITH STEPS

1. Learn to see the world through the lens of your child.

2. Let gentleness communicate your love even when your child fails.

3. Be sensitive to the influence of your words on the emotional development of your child.

4. Keep your child from losing heart.

5. Don't be too proud to say, "I am sorry."

6. Regularly affirm your child's positive attributes.

7. Create opportunities for your child to be successful every day.

A PARENT'S PRAYER

Father, Help me to be sensitive to the wonderfully delicate heart of my child. Guard my tongue from saying things that wound my child's spirit. Hold my hands back from causing him physical harm or injury. I want to use my words and actions to show my child how important he is to You and to me. I want my child to have confidence because my life has been an illustration of personal peace and security. Amen.

PARENTING INSIGHTS

SPECIAL CARE INSTRUCTIONS

Research Highlight: Your Child and Trauma

Jill Riethmayer offers some insights on trauma that may help you meet your child's emotional needs more effectively. These comments are taken from an article she published in a recent issue of *Christian Counseling Today.*

> *Children of all ages feel the fear and anxiety that follow in the wake of a trauma; however, trauma is distinctly unique in its impact upon children. Children don't grasp the nature of trauma in the same manner as adults. Unlike adults, children have neither the ability to exert control over their immediate environment nor the ability to cognitively process the traumatic event. This makes trauma an extremely more terrifying event for the child.*[1]

Later, in the same article, Riethmayer points out that in many cases the possible result is that the traumatic experience will slow down the child's normal psychological, emotional, and cognitive development. If this occurs, the parent may observe the child responding with a sense of fear and helplessness that may result in disorganized, agitated, or regressed behavior. Also, the parent may see a number of other behaviors, such as separation anxiety, clinging behavior, startle responses, regression behaviorally, and loss of ability to control aggressive behavior. As the child continues to deal with the trauma, he may have flashbacks, lose interest and pleasure in enjoyable activities, retell the event many times, withdraw from other people, have sleep-related difficulties, experience aches and pains, and misinterpret the cause and meaning of the trauma.

RESEARCH APPLICATIONS

Here are the things you should do to support your child if a major traumatic event occurs:

• Provide age-appropriate information about the traumatic incident.
• Give him a sense of safety and protection from further crisis.
• Make sure his world has predictability and stability.
• Nurture him and offer a strong level of security, physically and emotionally.
• Display patience and understanding as the child sorts out what he has experienced.

Your goal is to restore your child's sense of safety; his expectation that the people he encounters daily will be kind, predictable, and trustworthy is very important.

"A joyful heart is good medicine, but a broken spirit dries up the bones" (Proverbs 17:22).

Ask God to give you a way to lift your child's heart as he reacts to life after the trauma.

4

SEEK LONG-TERM INSURANCE

Meeting Your Child's Spiritual Needs

"Aren't we going to pray?"

Those were the words of my now oldest daughter at the home of a dear friend of ours who was gracious enough to keep our children overnight for us many years ago when we went out of town for ministry. Our friend had tucked my daughter into bed without a family prayer time.

When we heard what my daughter had said to our friend we were embarrassed and encouraged at the same time. We were encouraged because my daughter had gotten so accustomed to prayer before bedtime as a part of a family ritual that she didn't feel like her evening was complete until she participated in a family prayer. We were embarrassed because she blurted that out to our dear friend in the way she did.

After our friend related the story to us when we picked up our daughter, we were convinced that we needed to continue to make sure our children participated in a family conversation with God every day they were in our household. We don't feel like we can claim credit for the idea. God thought of it first.

A PARENT IS GOD'S GREATEST AND MOST IMPORTANT TEACHER

In fact, it is clearly communicated and illustrated in Deuteronomy 6:4–9.

> "Hear, O Israel! The Lord is our God, and the Lord is one! You shall love the Lord your God with all your heart and with all your soul and with all your might. These words, which I am commanding you today, shall be on your heart. You shall teach them diligently to your sons and shall talk of them when you sit in your house and when you walk by the way and when you lie down and when you rise up. You shall bind them as a sign on your hand and they shall be as frontals on your forehead. You shall write them on the doorposts of your house and on your gates."

What a great opportunity you have as a parent to use everyday encounters with your children to create a spiritual incubator to help them develop to the full potential God endowed them with when they were conceived and then born into the world. You have an important role in the spiritual development of your children. It is wonderful that there are great teachers in the church and in Christian schools. But teaching your children about God is still your ultimate responsibility. How can you do that? That is not a simple question. But it is a first step in the process described in Deuteronomy 6:4–9.

TAKE CARE OF YOUR RELATIONSHIP WITH GOD

In the same passage, God instructs parents to teach their children spiritual truth. He also tells parents to take care of their relationship with Him first. The truth about God must be on the heart of the parent before it can become a part of the life of the child.

One person put it this way: You cannot take a person where you have not been yourself. That applies to your ability as a parent. If you don't have a dynamic relationship with God, it will be very difficult for you to help your child develop a strong relationship with God.

Your spiritual instruction of your children should be an overflow of your personal relationship with God as a parent. The life of the New Testament figure Timothy gives us a fascinating look at how a mother and grandmother who have a dynamic walk with God can impact the spiritual development of their children. The apostle Paul wrote to Timothy: "For I am mindful of the sincere faith within you, which first dwelt in your grandmother Lois and your mother Eunice, and I am sure it is in you as well" (2 Timothy 1:5). Your spiritual strength will be a reservoir out of which you can minister to and instruct your child. Build a deep and wide reservoir of spiritual maturity to draw from as you teach your child spiritual truth.

FOCUS PARENTALLY ON THE SPIRITUAL FORMATION OF YOUR CHILDREN

It is interesting that the Bible is speaking directly to you as a parent. The responsibility for taking care of the spiritual needs of your children is not relegated to any institution or to any individual outside your Christian home.

It is your responsibility.

In our day of hectic schedules and demanding jobs, it is not uncommon for a parent to depend on the school and/or the church to help him with this responsibility. But that will not be enough. The spiritual needs of your children are a 24/7 responsibility. That means twenty-four hours a day seven days a week you have the privilege and responsibility of shepherding the growth and development of your child spiritually.

There is no reason why you cannot delegate some of the tasks associated with that responsibility to your church or school. Some churches have some dynamic programs to teach children the Bible. You would be wise to take full advantage of the resources available in your local church.

But it is still your responsibility.

Churches and schools are intended to play a supplementary role in the process of teaching your children about God; they are not to become a substitute for your work. Carefully balance how you rely on influences outside of your home for the things you should do yourself personally. Don't give away this wonderful privilege to a person who did not bring your child into the world.

INTRODUCE YOUR CHILD TO A PERSONAL RELATIONSHIP WITH GOD

Well, it would be great if your child knows how to think, speak, write, and serve. All those things are very important. But they pale in comparison with making sure that your child has many opportunities to respond to the message of the gospel of Jesus Christ.

Tell her about Jesus yourself. Help her understand the difference between being religious and having a personal relationship with God. But don't stop there. Expose her to gospel presentations in every possible forum that you can.

Make sure she understands God's love for her above all. A classic passage of Scripture that will help you communicate this truth is John 3:16: "For God so loved the world, that He gave His only begotten Son, that whoever believes in Him shall not perish, but have eternal life." It is important that you lay the foundation of God's love in a way that leaves no doubt in your child's mind. Otherwise, your child faces the ever-present danger of becoming religious but not enjoying the wonder of a personal relationship with God.

After you establish your child's understanding of God's love for her, it is critical that she understands her need for a Savior. This means you have to help her understand the concept of sin.

Be very careful here. It is important to help your child understand that all people are sinners. Romans 3:23–24 gives a clear statement of the biblical view of sin. "For all have sinned and fall short of the glory of God, being justified as a gift by His grace through the redemption which is in Christ Jesus."

You don't have to be harsh to communicate this concept. Just let your child know that since only God is perfect, all our negative behavior falls short of His perfect standard of holiness. There are many ways you can illustrate this by helping your child recognize that things like lying, hitting, taking things that don't belong to her, and even thinking bad thoughts about people are all sin. That will help her avoid the temptation to get in a judging posture where she judges her peers in an unhealthy way.

Once your child understands that she, like you and everyone else, is a sinner, teach her the beauty of God's grace. Help her understand that God knows that she needs Him and has provided the means through grace for her to come to know Him in a personal way. Paul captured that idea in Ephesians 2:8–9. "For by grace you have been saved through faith; and that not of yourselves, it is the gift of God; not as a result of works, so that no one may boast."

It was this verse of Scripture that helped me understand that no matter how hard I worked, it would not be good enough to earn my way into heaven. That helped me understand that I needed a Savior. I understood I couldn't save myself.

That verse also helped me understand that salvation is a gift from God. This is one of the most important truths you can give to your child—her personal salvation is a gift from God. Salvation is a free gift of God. If your child understands that salvation is a free gift, she will be anxious to understand how she can receive that free gift from God.

When your child recognizes that she cannot work her way into heaven, you have the wonderful privilege of making it clear that this free gift of salvation is found in Jesus Christ. Romans 6:23 gives a plain statement of this spiritual truth: "For the wages of sin is death, but the free gift of God is eternal life in Christ Jesus our Lord." Salvation comes through the gift of God given in Jesus Christ our Lord. Don't confuse your child by making her think that if she is "good enough" God will accept her into heaven. You need to make sure she understands how to accept Jesus as her personal Savior.

There are many verses in the Bible that illustrate the simplicity of that truth. One verse I find clear and appropriate for communicating to a child is Romans 10:9–10: "If you confess with your mouth Jesus as Lord, and believe in your heart that God raised Him from the dead, you will be saved."

This verse focuses on Jesus as the center and key to salvation and in the heart as the place a child expresses her commitment to Jesus Christ. Guide your child through the process of giving her heart to Jesus through a prayer that allows her to express her personal faith in Jesus Christ.

ASSURE YOUR CHILD THAT HER SALVATION IS SECURE IN JESUS CHRIST

Undoubtedly, your child will not always feel like she deserves to go to heaven. Sometimes she will make mistakes that cause her deep pain and frustration. In those times of personal failure, she could begin to doubt her salvation. That's why it is very important that you help her understand that her salvation is not secure because she does good things but because she has placed her faith in Jesus Christ.

First John 5:11–13 gives a clear understanding of the security of salvation for you and your children: "And the testimony is this, that God has given us eternal life, and this life is in His Son. He who has the Son has the life; he who does not have the Son of God does not have the life."

One way to communicate this powerful truth is to let your child know that she did not earn her salvation and cannot keep her salvation by her behavior. Instead, remind her over and over again that her salvation is secure because of her personal relationship with Jesus Christ.

GIVE YOUR CHILD WAYS TO KEEP HER RELATIONSHIP WITH GOD STRONG

Once your child has made a commitment to Jesus Christ, you have the opportunity to make sure she nurtures her relationship with God. One of the ways you can do that is to encourage your child to learn about God through reading the Bible on a daily basis. First Peter 2:2–3 says, "Like newborn babies, long for the pure milk of the word, so that by it you may grow in respect to salvation, if you have tasted the kindness of the Lord."

Help your child understand that just as she needs physical food to keep her physical body strong, so she needs to read the Bible to make sure she stays strong spiritually. Building this habit into your child's life at an early age will be a tremendous gift to her.

There are many different ways you can help your child develop the habit of reading her Bible on a daily basis. Over the years we have used a number of different approaches. If you have a good Christian bookstore nearby, they will most likely have books and resources designed to help you do that.

The method you use is not nearly as important as the practice of consistently modeling and encouraging your child to develop a love for the Scriptures. Why is that true? Well, there are a number of reasons. But one of the main reasons is that the Bible will give her the direction she needs to make wise daily decisions. The psalmist makes a personal declaration that is true for you and your child. "Your word is a lamp to my feet and a light to my path" (Psalm 119:105).

You will find no better source of instruction for teaching your child how to deal with the daily challenges and opportunities of the future than the Bible. One of the regular questions I ask my children is, "What is God teaching you lately?" Hopefully, this practice among other things will keep them focused on the importance of their personal spiritual growth.

TEACH YOUR CHILD HOW TO PRAY

Prayer is not some mystical experience that can only be done by very spiritual adults. Prayer is simply talking with God. Show and tell that to your child. Guide her to understand that she can talk with God just like you and any other adult can.

Spend time every day praying with your children. Jesus gave His disciples a model prayer to help them know how to communicate with God.

> "Pray, then, in this way:
> 'Our Father who is in heaven,
> Hallowed be Your name.
> Your kingdom come,
> Your will be done,
> On earth as it is in heaven.
> Give us this day our daily bread.
> And forgive us our debts, as we also have forgiven our debtors.
> And do not lead us into temptation, but deliver us from evil. [For Yours is the kingdom and the power and the glory forever. Amen.]'"
>
> —Matthew 6:9–13

Maybe you could consider beginning and ending each day with a brief word of prayer with your child. For our family, it has been a simple prayer at the beginning and end of each day as bookmarks that point toward heaven. A ritual of daily family prayer will help your child understand that talking with God is not something you do just in religious services only; rather, it is something you do as a part of your daily experience.

When you teach and lead your child to develop a life of prayer, it will help her do several things:

1. Affirm God's place of authority over her life instead of earthly values.
2. Adore God's person and His holiness over herself.

3. Accept God's prerogative to elevate kingdom priorities over personal preferences.
4. Ask for God to provide rather than depend on her own resources and ability.
5. Attend to the need to keep short accounts with God in areas of personal failure.
6. Access God's power to engage in the spiritual battle on a regular basis.
7. Acknowledge her primary purpose for existence is to give glory to God.

If your child can develop these deep roots of prayer while she is in your home, it could produce fruit in her life for a lifetime. This personal interaction through daily praying together will also build a strong relationship between you and your child.

TEACH YOUR CHILD HOW TO KEEP SHORT ACCOUNTS WITH GOD

Your child will sin. Another way of saying that is to say that she will fall short of God's standard for her life. Just like you do. If that is true—and it is—it is very important that you help your child understand the importance of confessing her shortcomings to God so that she can keep a pure heart. When your child does not learn to quickly acknowledge personal failings, it can lead to an unnecessary burden from a sense of guilt. David described the impact not confessing sin will have on the person who hides his failure.

> How blessed is he whose transgression is forgiven,
> Whose sin is covered!
> How blessed is the man to whom the Lord does not impute iniquity,
> And in whose spirit there is no deceit!
>
> When I kept silent about my sin, my body wasted away
> Through my groaning all day long.
> For day and night Your hand was heavy upon me;
> My vitality was drained away as with the fever heat of summer.

I acknowledged my sin to You,
And my iniquity I did not hide;
I said, "I will confess my transgressions to the Lord";
And You forgave the guilt of my sin.

—Psalm 32:1–5

When a child does not know the importance of keeping her heart pure before God, she can find herself in a form of spiritual and emotional bondage, as David described in Psalm 32.

I remember hearing a powerful story about a young boy who went along with his sister to visit their grandmother on a farm during the summer. It was a treasured experience full of all kinds of activities they did not enjoy at home. They also had a very loving grandmother.

One afternoon during the course of their visit, the young boy was throwing rocks and hit one of his grandmother's chickens in the backyard. Much to the surprise of the young boy and his sister, the chicken died. He did not intend to hit the chicken on its head. The young boy was shocked and hurriedly buried the chicken in the backyard and continued to play.

Little did he know that covering up that incident would cause him grief for days to come.

When they had finished eating supper, the little boy jumped up from his seat to go outside and play. As he got up, his sister called him back and with a real attitude of authority told him, "You are going to wash dishes tonight." He could tell by the look in her face that it was either dishes or she would tell.

This happened three consecutive nights. Finally, the little boy got tired of having to deal with the bondage of the secret they shared about the chicken he had killed. He was determined that he was not going to wash the dishes, no matter what.

On the third night, when they were out playing, his sister said to him, "You know you have to wash the dishes again."

The young boy responded, "I'm not going to wash the dishes."

The sister resorted to her now very familiar threat. "I'm going to tell Grandma."

The boy blurted out, "No, you are not, because I'm going to tell her myself!"

As they raced to the house to their grandmother, the boy began to cry and tell her how he was throwing rocks and killed the chicken. He said at the end of his confession, “I’m sorry, Grandma.”

His grandmother said to him, “I know you killed the chicken. I was sitting at the window watching when it happened. The part that hurt me the most was that you didn’t come to me and admit you did it earlier. I forgive you.”

One of the most important truths we can teach our children is that God is sitting at the window of heaven watching their every move. He is not surprised by their sin. Remind them of that comforting passage, 1 John 1:9: “If we confess our sins, He is faithful and righteous to forgive us our sins and to cleanse us from all unrighteousness.”

Tell them that God sees their sin and He wants them to come to Him and admit their failure. And most important of all, let them know that He will forgive them and clean them up on the inside if they admit they have failed.

TEACH YOUR CHILD HOW TO FELLOWSHIP WITH OTHER BELIEVERS

I love the lessons we learn from a charcoal grill. You say, “What lesson is that?” Well, have you ever tried to keep a charcoal grill burning with one piece of charcoal? Of course not. You need several pieces in that grill to keep them all burning. That principle applies to our spiritual lives.

That is one of the reasons fellowship with other believers in a local church is so important. It gives us the extra warmth we need to keep going within a system of accountability. The writer of the book of Hebrews communicated an admonition you need to weave into the fabric of your child’s regular experience. “Let us consider how to stimulate one another to love and good deeds, not forsaking our own assembling together, as is the habit of some, but encouraging one another; and all the more as you see the day drawing near” (Hebrews 10:24–25).

TEACH YOUR CHILD HOW TO GIVE AND SERVE

You have a wonderful opportunity to help your children gain the wonderful benefits of sharing their gifts and resources with others. One of the most compelling quotes I have ever read was written on a little plaque with these words.

> "Those who bring sunshine into the lives of others cannot keep it from themselves."

Although our child's motivation should not be to give in order to get, God's Word makes it clear that when we give our gifts and resources to Him it will result in His blessing our efforts. God has given some clear illustrations that can be used to teach your children the power of service and their potential to make an impact for God through their availability. John 6 gives a wonderful window into God's capacity to take what each of us has, including our children, and multiply it for the benefit of other people for His glory.

> Now the Passover, the feast of the Jews, was near. Therefore Jesus, lifting up His eyes and seeing that a large crowd was coming to Him, said to Phillip, "Where are we to buy bread, so that these may eat?" This He was saying to test him, for He Himself knew what He was intending to do. Phillip answered Him, "Two hundred denarii worth of bread is not sufficient for them, for everyone to receive a little." One of His disciples, Andrew, Simon Peter's brother, said to Him, "There is a lad here who has five barley loaves and two fish, but what are these for so many people?" Jesus said, "Have the people sit down." Now there was much grass in the place. So the men sat down, in number about five thousand. Jesus then took the loaves, and having given thanks, He distributed to those who were seated; likewise also of the fish as much as they wanted. (John 6:4–11)

Help your children understand that God simply wants them to serve the Lord by making their resources available for His use. Shaping the way they handle their treasures, toys, and time will help them develop very significant habits that will honor God as a child and well into their adult life. Here are a few concrete suggestions:

- Teach them to regularly give to the Lord's work at church during the weekly offering time.
- If opportunities exist for them to serve in the church, encourage them to take full advantage of those opportunities.

- Regularly encourage them to give away toys they no longer use.
- Clear their closets of clothing they can't wear anymore and let them give them away to people who are less fortunate.
- Give them special opportunities to serve people who are facing challenging situations, such as the homeless, and other similar situations under appropriate supervision.

If you apply these simple suggestions by modeling and instructing as a parent, it will be a real boost to the spiritual development of your child. I should emphasize that one of the most important parts of teaching your children how to serve is to make sure that they learn to give and serve not for credit or compliments but for Christ. That will greatly increase the possibility of their service being part of their daily routine rather than religious ritual.

USE EVERYDAY LIFE EXPERIENCES AS THE GREATEST CLASSROOM

Research and experience teaches that a young child forms her impression of God by watching the example of her parents. When your child hears the word *God,* the most powerful subconscious image she will associate with that word is the example she has experienced with your life. What a sobering thought. A parent has the awesome responsibility to give his or her child an image of God. Helping your child lay a solid spiritual foundation is strongly connected with the power of your personal example. Edgar Guest captured the power and simplicity of the influence you can have through a life well lived in front of your children.

SERMONS WE SEE

By Edgar Guest

I'd rather see a sermon than hear one any day.
I'd rather one should walk with me than merely show the way.
The eye's a better pupil and more willing than the ear;
Fine counsel is confusing, but example's always clear;
And the best of all the preachers are the men who love their creeds,
For to see the good in action is what everybody needs.

I can soon learn how to do it if you'll let me see it done.
I can watch your hands in action, but your tongue too fast may run.
And the lectures you deliver may be very wise and true;
But I'd rather get my lesson by observing what you do.
For I may misunderstand you and the high advice you give,
But there is no misunderstanding how you act and how you live.[1]

FAITH STEPS

1. Pray with and for your child (personal relationship with and commitment to God) on a daily basis.

2. Seize formal and informal opportunities to teach your child spiritual truth on a regular basis.

3. Challenge your child to apply the Scripture she is learning in fresh ways every day.

4. Involve your child in regular interaction with a group of peers who will reinforce the values God has prioritized.

5. Expose your child to positive Christian mentors and fill your child's life with illustrations and images that point her to a vibrant personal relationship with God.

A PARENT'S PRAYER

Father, Thank You for giving me the opportunity to teach my child spiritual truth every day. Keep my heart bent toward You so that I can access Your strength and power each day through prayer. Help me to expose my child to godly role models who will provide additional instruction and examples of godliness for her. Open my child's heart so that she can experience a personal relationship and a dynamic walk with You every day. Amen.

PARENTING INSIGHTS

SPECIAL CARE INSTRUCTIONS

Research Highlight: Your Child and Music

Music can be a useful tool to enhance your child's intellectual, social, emotional, and spiritual development. Here are some basic facts from research that may stimulate your creativity and ideas for ways you can use music to strengthen your parental effectiveness.

RESEARCH HIGHLIGHTS

- Music connects the right and left hemispheres of the brain, thereby enhancing learning.
- Music enhances creativity.
- Music reduces stress.
- Different styles and types of music can be used to elicit a variety of emotional responses in children.
- Music heightens emotional involvement in learning and helps store and retrieve multisensory memories.
- Repetition, rhyme, and rhythm associated with music can enhance a child's ability to remember facts.[2]

These research results provide the basis for some really creative uses of music to help your child develop to his full personal potential.

RESEARCH APPLICATIONS

1. Use music to nurture the emotional development of your child from the womb to adulthood.
2. Teach your child to enjoy a wide variety of musical styles.
3. Use music to help calm your child down during high stress situations.

4. Creatively use music to help teach your child important spiritual concepts.

5. Keep a wide variety of Christian music on hand to encourage your child to listen to positive musical messages.

6. Help your child identify themes and ideas that are subtle attacks on the message of the Bible.

7. Equip your child with the level of discernment he needs to filter music that doesn't contribute to his spiritual maturity.

"Let our Lord now command your servants who are before you. Let them seek a man who is a skillful player on the harp; and it shall come about when the evil spirit from God is on you, that he shall play the harp with his hand, and you will be well" (1 Samuel 16:16).

Use the medium of music to your advantage in an effort to cultivate godly character in the life of your child and enable him to enjoy his personal relationship with God.

5

HEAVENLY SPECIFICATIONS

Your Child's Growth and Development

One grandmother asked her friend, "How old are your grandchildren?" Her friend replied, "The teacher is two years old, and the minister is four years old." That was a cute conversation at best, because neither woman really knew what the future was for her grandchild. But it sure didn't keep the two ladies from speculating and dreaming.

Those grandmothers were like every parent who has the privilege of caring for another life. One of the greatest mysteries of the parenting process is waiting for the answer to the question, *What will my child become?* No doubt you have dreams for the future of your child. Every parent does. But God doesn't always give a quick response.

Most puzzles have a picture of the finished project on the outside of the box. Most model airplanes come with a diagram showing what the plane looks like when it is all put together, with step-by-step instructions. Yet when our children are born, we don't receive the kind of instructions you get with a puzzle or model airplane.

MADE TO HEAVENLY SPECIFICATIONS

Although we don't get pictures of what their lives will look like at maturity or step-by-step instructions at their births, God gives us insights in Scripture as to what is on the inside of the beautiful gift and life He gives us in our children. It is fascinating to review some of the things the Scripture says about our children.

Once you see your child completely from God's perspective, you will never look at your privilege of parenting in the same way. That's why, over the next few pages, I want to tell you what the Bible says about people in general and children in particular. You will learn some intriguing things about your child.

Earlier in this book we shared a number of truths about your child:

- Your child was created in the image of God.
- Your child was made by the pattern of a divine blueprint.
- You child was given to you as a gift.
- God made your child irreplaceable and unrepeatable.

Now we want to share a few additional insights about this special gift God has given you. Once you understand the wonderful artistry of God displayed in your child, it will cause you to marvel at the wonderful gift He has given you in the life of your child.

Your child is a multidimensional person

You clearly see the physical dimension of your child, but when the Bible describes each one of us—including our children—it makes clear that we are far more complex than what the naked eye can see. That scriptural truth is reflected in the prayer of Paul for the Thessalonian believers: "Now may the God of peace Himself sanctify you entirely: and may your spirit and soul and body be preserved complete, without blame at the coming of our Lord Jesus Christ" (1 Thessalonians 5:23).

A child as a person is made of multiple dimensions that include body, soul, and spirit. It's amazing, isn't it, that God is concerned about the total person. So each of us as a parent should be committed to the development of our child's total person.

Your child's body is a temple of the Holy Spirit

The Bible makes it clear that a believer has the responsibility of treating his body as an instrument to glorify God. "Or do you not know that your body is a temple of the Holy Spirit who is in you, whom you have from God, and that you are not your own? For you have been bought with a price: therefore glorify God in your body" (1 Corinthians 6:19–20).

You have the privilege of helping your child understand at the earliest possible age the importance of taking care of his body. What a great gift you can give your child by helping him establish healthy habits early.

We have had at least two family experiences that have given us deep convictions about our diet and routine as a family when it relates to physical well-being. During my youngest daughter's earliest years of life, she had to make a lot of visits to the hospital because of some serious health problems. After she had experienced at least eight hospitalizations and countless exams, our doctors discovered that my daughter had a metabolic disorder that was agitated by fat in her diet. Due to this metabolic disorder, even a small amount of fat in her diet caused her great pain and discomfort. A change in her diet literally changed her life.

While my daughter's problems were complicated by a metabolic disorder, we learned how destructive excessive amounts of fat can be to a healthy child. We were convinced more than ever that our children's diet was important. Similarly, your child's diet will have an impact on his current level of health and future well-being.

My wife's recent battle with breast cancer has also caused us to have a heightened level of awareness of how important it is to care for our bodies and to help our children understand the importance of being good stewards of their physical well-being. When Annie was first diagnosed with breast cancer, we researched every available source to find ways to contribute to her health and recovery. That process resulted in some life-changing insights for us about the impact our daily habits have on our health. Although Annie has always provided healthy, nutritious meals for our family, her illness took us to a deeper level of conviction about the importance of diet.

Dr. Michael Jacobson in chapter 6 of *The Word on Health* offers some medical advice that also reflects his understanding of scriptural principles. He lists ten different strategies.

1. Eat only what you need.
2. Obtain adequate exercise.
3. Eat "real" food.
4. Make plant food the foundation of your diet.
5. Drink pure water.
6. Prefer "clean" animal flesh.
7. Don't eat blood or improperly prepared food.
8. Don't eat the "hard" fat of animals.
9. Culture your dairy products.
10. Don't let diet take precedence over God or others.[1]

This advice provides a firm foundation for teaching your child so that his diet reflects practical wisdom and sensitivity to God's instruction to believers through Scripture.

In addition to the advice from Dr. Jacobson and numerous other nutrition experts, I have developed what I call "A Comprehensive Plan for Total Wellness." My personal goal is to slowly move toward this pattern of living. My dream is to model for my children a pattern of living they will embrace as God leads them. It will be fun to see what happens.

Some of you may consider this comprehensive plan a little obsessive. Relax. Follow your own convictions about your family's diet. Although the elements of my plan are well researched, these observations don't rise to the level of Scripture. Use the elements of the plan as God leads you. I offer this overview of some personal research for your benefit.

If you want to do all you can to make sure your child experiences optimal health, know that some major elements keep surfacing as foundational. Let me share them with you in summary form.

- Make sure your child's diet is balanced.
- Try to help your child develop a routine that includes an adequate amount of rest.
- Keep your child active so that exercise is a routine part of his life experience.
- Finally, guide your child to take care of himself through sound health practices.

A COMPREHENSIVE PLAN FOR TOTAL WELLNESS

Dietary Restrictions

- *Limit Processed Sugar*
- *Limit Refined Flour*
- *Limit Saturated Fat*
- *Limit Dairy Products*
- *Limit Caffeine*
- *Limit Alcohol*

Sample Healthy Foods

- *Vegetables (Dark Green, Cruciferous, etc.)*
- *Soy Products (Tofu, Quinoa, etc.)*
- *Beans, Legumes*
- *Grains, Seeds, and Nuts*
- *Whole Fruit/Juices (Carrot, Citrus, Apple, etc.)*

Healthy Supplements

- *Take a Good Multivitamin Daily*
- *Take Vitamin C/Antioxidants Daily*
- *Take Mineral Supplements Daily*
- *Enhance Diet with Natural Herbs/Spices*
- *Supplement Diet for Individual Needs*

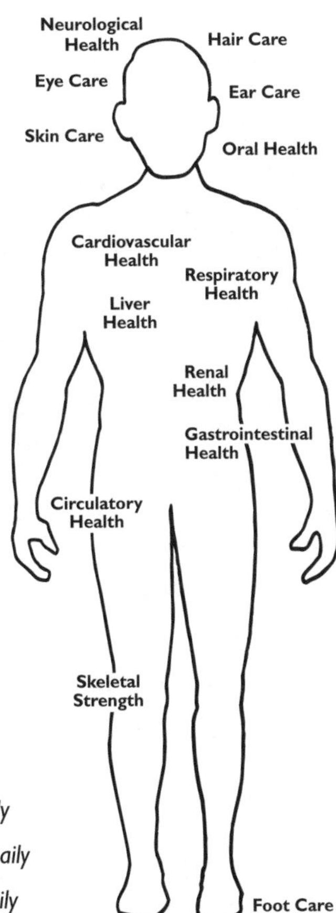

Dietary Goals

- *Eat Fruits and Vegetables*
- *Consume High Fiber Diet*
- *Consume Low Fat Diet*
- *Consume Vitamins and Minerals*
- *8 Glasses of Water Daily*
- *Consume Essential Fats*

Good Intake Habits

- *Eat Live Foods*
- *Chew Foods Thoroughly*
- *Combine Foods Properly*
- *Care for Digestive System*
- *Boost Immune System*

Personal Habits

- *Exercise 30 Minutes Daily*
- *Eliminate Regularly*
- *Rest Body Adequately*
- *Engage in Positive Activities*
- *Practice Good Personal Hygiene*

Healthy Beverages

- *Fruit Juices*
- *Soy/Rice Milk*
- *Herbal Drinks, Green Teas*
- *Water*
- *Vegetable Drinks*

Essential Fat Sources

- *Dark Green Leafy Vegetables*
- *Cold Pressed Oils (Flax, etc.)*
- *Nuts, Seeds*
- *Salmon, Tuna*
- *Herring*

Healthy Snacks

- *Berries, Raisins, Dates*
- *Yogurt, Soy Products*
- *Vegetables (Carrots/Celery)*
- *Fruit Slices (Bananas, Apples, etc.)*
- *Nuts, Seeds*

Your child's emotional makeup is part of his person

The physical part of your child's life is easy to distinguish, but what you can't see as easily is the emotional dimension of your child. On the inside of your child's body is a complex web that makes up his emotional side. It's the emotional side of the child that erupts into a temper tantrum when things don't go his way or breaks into a generous smile when he is happy. My oldest daughter reflected the power of emotions expressed through the form of a simple smile in this poem she wrote a number of years ago.

A SMILE

What makes your day the best,
Even when nothing has gone as planned?
What reflects love and care for a person?
What brings light to your life even in the darkest night?
What can express what words could never let anyone know?
A smile.

Emotions at their root are simply impulses to act. God has created us to respond to our environment. So if anything threatens our safety, we retreat or take action to protect ourselves. God has also wired us to display tenderness and warmth when we feel secure and comfortable. Equipping your child to control his impulses to act, especially expressing anger, will be one of the greatest contributions you can make to his life. "He who is slow to anger is better than the mighty, and he who rules his spirit, than he who captures a city" (Proverbs 16:32).

Some impulses direct a child to do positive, productive things. Other impulses lead a child toward self-destructive behavior. Your challenge is to help your child recognize and control those impulses so that he keeps himself healthy emotionally. The psalmist captures the importance of keeping the soul and spirit strong: "Watch over your heart with all diligence, for from it flow the springs of life" (Proverbs 4:23).

We know from Scripture that a person's emotional state is important. "Hope deferred makes the heart sick, but desire fulfilled is a tree of life" (Proverbs 13:12). That is why you need to understand as much as you can about what helps a child develop emotional strength and security. Indeed, some of the latest research seems to indicate that a person's EQ (Emotional Quotient) is as critical to his success as his IQ (Intellectual Quotient).[2]

Sensitivity to your child's natural fears
is an important part of the parental process

It is important for you to know the fears your child faces. You have a great opportunity to minister to your children by being sensitive to the reality of their fears and by responding with kindness and strength. Let them know that you recognize their need for encouragement. Don't minimize the legitimacy of their fears. Instead, assure them of God's power and your personal presence as a way to help them feel a sense of security.

THE FEARS OF CHILDHOOD

INFANT–TODDLER FEARS

Fear of abandonment
Fear of being overpowered
Fear of losing parental love and approval
Oedipal fears (competition with the same-sex parent for the love of the opposite-sex parent)

LATE PRESCHOOLER FEARS

Fear of the power of "big people" to inflict pain
Fear of nightmares and night terrors

GRADE-SCHOOLER FEARS

Fear of competing and losing in life
Fear of being insignificant and without value
Fear of sexuality

TEENAGE FEARS

Fear of growing up
Fear of liberation and independence
Fear of new situations and new challenges

Source: Frank Minirth, Paul Meier, Stephen Arterburn, *The Complete Life Encyclopedia* (Nashville: Thomas Nelson, 1995), 292.

Teach them that although their fears are real, they are not from God. "For God has not given us a spirit of timidity, but of power and love and discipline" (2 Timothy 1:7). The chart "The Fears of Childhood" outlines the different fears of each age group.

God gives power and confidence in the midst of challenge. You have the wonderful privilege of helping your child understand and gain confidence in God through his times of fear.

The roots of healthy emotional development are important

Unless your child has special needs in this area, you can help him stay emotionally healthy mainly by making sure several keys to emotional health are part of his life experience. Create as many avenues of personal success for your child as possible. Affirming relationships are an important tool to help him develop confidence in himself. Help him to have repeated experiences of personal success. Then when he has to deal with pain and loss, make sure he has support during those difficult times.

Your child has an intellectual dimension of his person

One of the most powerful growth periods I have had was when I was doing research for this book. The things I have learned about the human personality have been fascinating. One aspect of that fascination has been the power and significance of the human mind, especially the growth of the brain. Your child's brain is a complex creation of God that fuels and directs every other part of his body.

It is no wonder that God places such a significant focus on the mind in the Scripture. In order for your child to apply the truth of Romans 12:2, you need to do everything you can to make sure his intellectual capacity is as sharp as possible. "And do not be conformed to this world, but be transformed by the renewing of your mind, so that you may prove what the will of God is, that which is good and acceptable and perfect."

Your child's brain will not grow by accident or osmosis. It happens best when a parent engages in an intentional process to help his child reach his full human potential by making sure his child has the best of what his resources can offer, especially during the early formative years. How do you do that?

- Provide stimulating reading material so that your child will develop a love for reading and learning.
- Encourage your child to listen to wholesome music that will broaden his perspective and interface with the world.
- Engage your child in interesting conversation by talking about current events in his life, the life of the family, and his world.
- Help your child develop a mental filter that will screen out thinking patterns that will lead him away from God.
- Start when he is young by talking about the kinds of thinking patterns that will work against his present success and short-circuit his future.

Your child's maturity occurs through a systematic process

The life of Jesus Christ illustrated that in the life of every person growth and development happen through a systematic process from childhood to adulthood. "Jesus kept increasing in wisdom and stature, and in favor with God and men" (Luke 2:52). Your child will be no exception. His physical, intellectual, spiritual, and social growth will be slow and steady. It is important that you try to stimulate that growth as much as possible.

We also can learn a lot about your child's development from science. The chart "Stages of Child Development" gives some idea of the patterns of growth children follow as they mature.

Be a student of how your child grows and matures as an individual. These patterns are just general guidelines to help you measure his growth in relationship to other children his age.

Your child has a need for a positive and strong social support system

Your child's relationships are critical. In fact, Scripture gives a clear warning to all believers about how we handle our social relationships.

> How blessed is the man who does not walk in the counsel of the wicked,
> Nor stand in the path of sinners,
> Nor sit in the seat of scoffers!
> But his delight is in the law of the Lord,
> And in His law he meditates day and night.

STAGES OF CHILD DEVELOPMENT

Age Period	**Major Developments**
Prenatal stage (conception to birth)	Basic body structure and organs form. Physical growth is most rapid in life span. Vulnerability to environmental influences is great.
Infancy and toddlerhood (Birth to age 3)	Newborn is dependent but competent. Physical growth and development of motor skills are rapid Ability to learn and remember is present, even in early weeks of life. Attachment to parents and others forms toward end of the first year. Self-awareness develops in second year. Comprehension and speech develop rapidly. Interest in other children increases.
Early childhood (3–6 years)	Family is still focus of life, although other children become more important. Fine and gross motor skills and strength improve. Independence, self-control, and self-care increase. Play, creativity, and imagination become more elaborate. Cognitive immaturity leads to many "illogical" ideas about the world. Behavior is largely egocentric, but understanding other people's perspective grows.
Middle childhood (6 to 12 years)	Peers assume central importance. Children begin to think logically, although largely concretely. Egocentrism diminishes. Memory and language skills increase. Cognitive gains improve ability to benefit from formal schooling. Self-concept develops, affecting self-esteem. Physical growth slows. Strength and athletic skills improve.
Adolescence (12 to about 20 years)	Physical changes are rapid and profound. Reproductive maturity arrives. Search for identity becomes central. Peer groups help to develop and test self-concept. Ability to think abstractly and use scientific reasoning develops. Adolescent egocentrism persists in some behavior. Relationships with parents are generally good.

Source: Diane E. Papalia and Sally Wendkos Olds, *Human Development,* Sixth Edition (New York: McGraw-Hill, 1995), 7.

He will be like a tree firmly planted by streams of water,
Which yields its fruit in its season
And its leaf does not wither;
And in whatever he does, he prospers.

—Psalm 1:1–3

The truth of that passage not only applies to you as a parent, but also impacts your child. Where your child spends his time is very important. Also, the people he chooses to associate with will make a huge impact on the person he ultimately becomes.

Don't underestimate your child's need for a support system to help him deal with his personal struggles. If your child feels lonely, he will be vulnerable to exploitation and can be hurt very easily. It is important that you use your platform as a parent to give attention to your child's need for friendship and other supportive relationships. Here are some ways you can do that.

- Model for your child the importance of building positive interpersonal relationships.
- Help your child choose friends who honor God.
- Make sure your child always has someone to lean on.

If you ignore the importance of your child's social relationships, you will make a critical mistake.

Focus on practicing good health practices to protect God's gift to you

The editors of *Teaching Home* magazine did an excellent job of summarizing the "Elements of Good Health":

1. **Nourishment.** "The food we eat must contain all the specific nutrients required for each of our body functions. A lack of one nutrient can have serious long-term consequences because the body is designed to use nutrients in combination, not separately."
2. **Water.** "Water is absolutely essential for life and health. It is recommended that we drink one-half ounce for each pound of our

body weight every day. (For example, a 130-pound person needs 65 ounces or about 8 cups.)"

3. **Air.** "We all have to breathe, but many of us could benefit by learning to breathe better. We should breathe deeply and empty our lungs more completely than most of us do. Exercise and posture can improve our breathing as well."
4. **Exercise.** "Our bodies were designed to move and work a good part of the time, not sit still all day. Unused muscles tend to atrophy and our lymph system depends on muscle movement for circulation of immune factors. Our bones also need to bear our weight to stay strong."
5. **Rest.** "We need adequate rest for our bodies to grow and repair themselves and for our minds to be refreshed. God ordained that we should rest from our work one day a week and that we should sleep every night. . . . A midday nap can effectively supplement our nightly sleep if it adds up to whatever total time our individual bodies need. This may be 7 hours for one person and 12 hours for another; we should sleep neither less than nor more than we need. Growing children, even teens, may need 11 or 12 hours of sleep, with or without an additional nap during the day."
6. **Hygiene.** "Many diseases can be avoided if we are habitually careful about cleanliness. It is especially important to wash hands often throughout the day in addition to regular washing of skin, hair, teeth, and clothes."
7. **Shelter.** "Besides a roof and walls to shelter us from cold, storms, rain, and snow, we also need protection from the sun and from attacks by animals and people."
8. **Safety.** "Accidents are a leading cause of death and disability as well as injury and illness, especially for children. For this reason, knowing and practicing safety rules is essential for health."
9. **Medicine.** "When we get sick, it is helpful to know some ways to treat the illness at home as well as if and when to consult a doctor and how to evaluate his advice."
10. **Morality.** "The most important consideration for any aspect of our physical lives is 'What would the Lord Jesus have us do?' If we study God's Word, we will have the wisdom and guidance in every area. Obeying God's directions to be temperate in eating;

> to be pure sexually; to forsake anger, bitterness, and worry; to work hard and rest regularly, and to be clean in body and in conscience will help to keep us healthy both physically and spiritually as we honor Him."[3]

I don't believe I could say it better than that.
Now let's go and do it.

FAITH STEPS

1. See your child as a person with physical, emotional, and social needs.

2. Take care of your child's needs to the best of your ability on a daily basis.

3. Provide your child with a balanced, nutritional diet on a regular basis.

4. Help your child develop a strong EQ (Emotional Quotient).

5. Create a positive network of family, friends, and other positive people to build a support system for your child.

A PARENT'S PRAYER

Father, Thank You for giving me a child with physical, emotional, and social needs. Help me give myself fully to meeting those needs through Your strength and power. Give me the wisdom I need to take care of the physical needs of my child so that he maintains optimum physical health. Keep my child emotionally strong. Provide my child with a strong social network so that he will never feel like he is alone. Guide me so that my child grows to his full personal potential. Amen.

PARENTING INSIGHTS

SPECIAL CARE INSTRUCTIONS

Research Highlight: Your Child and Obesity

Recent research points to some very important facts about childhood obesity like:

- Childhood obesity now threatens one of every three children with long-term health problems.
- The U.S. government estimates that approximately 6 million children are "fat enough" to place their health in jeopardy.

By now, you may be saying, So what? Well childhood obesity does make a real difference in how long the child lives and the quality of that life. Here are some facts published in the July 3, 2000, issue of *Newsweek* that may answer that question in relevant terms.

> *Children's impulses haven't changed much in recent decades. But social forces from the demise of home cooking to the rise of fast food and video technology, have converged to make them heavier. . . . Obese kids suffer both physically and emotionally throughout childhood, and those who remain heavy as adolescents tend to stay that way into adulthood. The resulting illnesses—diabetes, heart disease, high blood pressure, several cancers—now claim an estimated half million American lives each year, while costing us $100 billion in medical expenses and lost productivity. U.S. Agriculture Secretary Dan Glickman predicts that obesity will soon rival smoking as a cause of preventable death.*[4]

RESEARCH APPLICATIONS

Aside from some obvious steps you can take, like limiting your child's television and computer-game time, making sure he is more physically active and eating a proper diet, Linda Avallone provides some helpful suggestions for teaching our children proper nutrition in *Teaching Home* magazine. She suggests the following steps to parents to promote proper nutrition. These steps, along with some good old-fashioned self-discipline, will contribute a great deal to your child's health and well-being.

1. Teach by example.

2. Make changes gradually.

3. Choose healthy snacks.

4. Study food groups.

5. Read labels.

6. Learn about specific food-related biologic processes.

7. Collect information about nutrition-related diseases.[5]

"Or do you not know that your body is a temple of the Holy Spirit who is in you, whom you have from God, and that you are not your own? For you have been bought with a price: therefore glorify God in your body" (1 Corinthians 6:19–20).

Give high priority to your child's personal care and dietary habits to promote the best possible health.

6

POWER SOURCE

Strength for Biblical Parenting

I enjoy going to the bookstore and reviewing book titles, especially those that deal with parenting. The titles are inviting. They read something like this:

- "How to Guarantee Holy, Happy Children"
- "Risk-free Parenting"
- "No More Problems with Your Children"
- "Painless Childrearing"
- "Ten Easy Steps to Raising Children Who Don't Sin"

Very attractive, but after more than twenty years as a parent and more than twenty-three years working with families in some professional context, I have concluded that they are just titles. I am sure the authors and publishers are well intentioned. But I am also equally sure that if they believe their books' contents can produce problem-free parenting for every person who reads them, then they can't deliver on what they have promised.

LIFE IS COMPLEX

Sometimes when I read those titles, laughter erupts. On other occasions, I frown. It all depends on my mood. Most of the time I reflect on the reality that life is just too complex to buy into simple formulas that only work when all the circumstances fall perfectly into place. Some people are fortunate enough for that to occur. For those people, maybe a few easy formulas will do. But most parents experience circumstances like the ones described in the Scripture.

> But realize this, that in the last days difficult times will come. For men will be lovers of self, lovers of money, boastful, arrogant, revilers, disobedient to parents, ungrateful, unholy, unloving, irreconcilable, malicious gossips, without self-control, brutal, haters of good, treacherous, reckless, conceited, lovers of pleasure rather than lovers of God. (2 Timothy 3:1–4)

Sound pessimistic? I pray not. I hope it points you in the right direction for your power and strength. Where do you find power in a world like that?

LOOK BEYOND YOURSELF FOR ULTIMATE STRENGTH

We are reminded in the book of Ephesians that though the battle for the hearts and minds of our children is fought on an earthly battlefield, the main weapons we have to be concerned about are not of this world. "For our struggle is not against flesh and blood, but against the rulers, against the powers, against the world forces of this darkness, against the spiritual forces of wicked in the heavenly places" (Ephesians 6:12).

That means that your starting point in practicing biblical parenting is to look beyond techniques, theories, and strategies for ultimate strength. Please don't misunderstand me. There are techniques and strategies that are very helpful. But don't ever get confused. That is not where the real power is.

I must confess to you that when I first started studying about parenting and presenting seminars almost eighteen years ago, my focus was more limited to techniques and strategies than I like to admit. Then my ministry expanded and my children started growing older. In short, I lived a little more life. I still believe in the benefits of most of the techniques I have been presenting over the years. But I am much more committed to the technique that no parenting expert ever created.

What is that technique?

It is *prayer.* Prayer should be the starting point for your power as a parent. I know you are really disappointed. You thought I would give you something profound and deep. Well, let me tell you that as parents we can't get any deeper than a commitment to the power of prayer. When counseling theories fail and techniques seem to cause more problems than solutions, prayer will always bring hope to the soul and peace to the spirit. Commit yourself to becoming a prayer warrior for your children. Call out their names to God every day asking for His mercy and protection. Let them hear you pray for them and with them.

What happens when you pray for and with your children? You will become closer to them and they will become closer to God. When Jesus' disciples asked Him how they should pray, He gave His disciples a model prayer that should be a guide for us in our prayers.

> "When you are praying, do not use meaningless repetition. . . . Pray then, in this way:
>
> 'Our Father who is in heaven,
> Hallowed be Your name.
> Your kingdom come.
> Your will be done,
> On earth as it is heaven.
> Give us this day our daily bread.
> And forgive us our debts, as we also have forgiven our debtors.
> And do not lead us into temptation, but deliver us from evil. [For Yours is the kingdom and the power and the glory forever. Amen.]'"
>
> —Matthew 6:7, 9–13

ACCESS POWER YOU CAN DEPEND ON

My ministry and professional experience have taken me behind prison walls, onto the grounds of juvenile institutions, to the campuses of schools, into the sanctuary of churches, and into the offices of professional social workers and counselors. I am certain of one thing. There are no easy human solutions or techniques that will solve everybody's problems. If there are no easy human solutions, where do we find answers that work?

Let me answer the question this way. I know an awful lot about parenting theories, approaches, and strategies. But I regularly fail to apply what I know when I rely on my own strength. That is why my confidence goes up immensely when I turn over everything to the Spirit of God when I get stumped. "But when He, the Spirit of truth, comes, He will guide you into all the truth; for He will not speak on His initiative, but whatever He hears, He will speak; and He will disclose to you what is to come" (John 16:13).

That is where I hope you go when you get stumped. There are times when you won't have a clue how to lead your child. God's Spirit is available to you as a source of guidance and strength in all facets of your life. During those times, one of the best things you can do is find a quiet place and pray. Simply agree with God about what He already knows: You don't have the power to raise your children in a way that will honor Him alone. But, remember, you don't have to.

KEEP SHORT ACCOUNTS WITH GOD

Sometimes God wants to speak to us, but our lives are so cluttered the Spirit can't speak: "If I regard wickedness in my heart, the Lord will not hear" (Psalm 66:18).

Don't let personal sin in your life block God's ability to speak with you. It is entirely possible that if you have unconfessed sin in your life, your influence on your children will be more negative than positive. I have found that when my spiritual arteries are clogged, it is very difficult for me to minister effectively to my children.

DEMONSTRATE A LIFE WORTH IMITATING

The most powerful tool you have apart from God's Word and the power of His Spirit is a life worth imitating. Your lifestyle is important. One of the important elements of the truth presented in Psalm 78 is the concept of "Show and Tell."

> Listen, O my people, to my instruction;
> Incline your ears to the words of my mouth.

I will open my mouth in a parable;
I will utter dark sayings of old,
Which we have heard and known,
And our fathers have told us.
We will not conceal them from their children,
But tell to the generation to come the praises of the Lord,
And His strength and His wondrous works that He has done.

For He established a testimony in Jacob
And appointed a law in Israel,
Which He commanded our fathers
That they should teach them to their children,
That the generations to come might know, even the children yet to be born,
That they may arise and tell them to their children.

—Psalm 78:1–6

Cultivating godly character in the lives of children involves illustrating as well as communicating spiritual commitment. Your consistent obedience to the truth of God's Word will be a powerful parental tool.

Unfortunately, the opposite is also true. If you present a poor example, it will short-circuit your effectiveness as a parent. I am not suggesting that you can offer a perfect life before your children. You can't. But it is important that your children don't have a valid reason for feeling like you are being hypocritical. Avoid the parental attitude that says, "Do as I say, not as I do." Instead, the most powerful parental attitude is "Follow me as I follow Christ." I love these simple words found on the tomb of an Anglican bishop.

> When I was young and free and my imagination had no limits, I dreamed of changing the world. As I grew older and wiser, I discovered the world would not change, so I shortened my sights somewhat and decided to change only my country.
>
> But it, too, seemed immoveable.
>
> As I grew into my twilight years, in one last desperate attempt, I settled for changing only my family, those closest to me, but alas, they would have none of it.

> And now as I lie on my deathbed, I suddenly realize: If I had only changed myself first, then by example I would have changed my family.
>
> From their inspiration and encouragement, I would then have been able to better my country and, who knows, I may have even changed the world.
>
> —Anonymous

Your visual witness before your children will create a platform for your verbal witness to your children.

DRAW UPON THE GRACE OF GOD

Don't forget that the grace of God is greater than your most glaring weaknesses and limitations. You will be wise to draw upon it. I will never forget one weekend seminar with a group of parents that made me realize how important it is to highlight this truth.

As I was sharing with this group of parents about the importance of parental example, I noticed one of the women near the back of the room had tears streaming down her face. I felt moved to approach her.

"Help me understand what you are feeling," I said to her. She responded, "If I had only known this before, I could have been a better parent." Then I told her what you should cling to as a source of strength when the Enemy reminds you of your weaknesses to discourage and disable you: "The grace of God is greater than your weakness." In 2 Corinthians the apostle Paul tells of a time when he prayed that God would remove a weakness from him. The reply he got was not what he had originally desired. "And He has said to me, 'My grace is sufficient for you, for power is perfected in weakness.' Most gladly, therefore, I will rather boast about my weaknesses, so that the power of Christ may dwell in me" (2 Corinthians 12:9).

I will always remember the look on her face when suddenly the responsibility of parenting became more real to her than it ever was before. At that moment she also realized her inadequacy in a way she never had before. She left that day understanding that when she came to the end of herself and reached out to God, she was touching only the beginning of the power available to her.

Please cling to that truth. The grace of God will give you power you don't possess to handle situations you cannot anticipate. As you parent your children, do the best you can, but never stop drawing upon the grace of God. When you start thinking you are sufficient and don't need God, you are in a dangerous position.

FAITH STEPS

1. Maintain a strong and vibrant personal relationship with God.
2. Keep short accounts with God so that the Holy Spirit can guide you.
3. Make prayer a regular part of your personal and family routine.
4. Develop accountable relationships with other Christian friends concerning your parenting practices.
5. Give your children a life worth imitating as a parent.

A PARENT'S PRAYER

Father, Thank You that I don't have the power to parent my child without You. I know that will make me trust You more. Lord, I want to seek Your power, not my own. Help me to pray diligently for my children. I am grateful as a Christian that Your Spirit lives within me to guide and direct me into Your truth. Clean my heart, O God, so that Your voice and will can be clear to me. I want so desperately to present a life worth imitating to my children. Lead me into the path of righteousness. I confess my weaknesses to You with a grateful heart that You accept in spite of my weakness. Willingly, I admit that without Your grace my efforts will fall short. And I rejoice in the truth that Your grace is sufficient to meet all my needs and all the challenges I will face. Amen.

PARENTING INSIGHTS

SPECIAL CARE INSTRUCTIONS

Research Highlight: Keys to School Success

One of the most important things a parent can do is to help her child achieve her personal potential intellectually and academically. There are foundational practices you can adopt to facilitate this growth.

RESEARCH HIGHLIGHTS

- Children learn best when they have nurturing, enriching environments that stimulate brain development and foster learning and personal growth.
- Children perform best when their physical, social, and emotional needs are met so that there are minimal distractions to the learning process.
- Children learn best when their personal environment is free of environmental toxins and other neurotoxins.
- Children learn best when their parents are actively involved in their learning and personal growth at school.
- Children learn best when they are in an environment that has high expectations of their capacity to learn and provides the tools and resources to facilitate maximum personal growth.
- Children learn best when a parent or caregiver has used music, singing, and play to expand their capacity to think creatively.
- Children learn best when their parents limit passive activities, such as television viewing, and replace them with activities that engage a child emotionally and promote intellectual stimulation.[1]

RESEARCH APPLICATIONS

1. Make sure your child has healthy nutritious meals and adequate rest every day so that she can perform up to her potential in school.

2. Cultivate your child's hunger for learning and exploration by talking and reading to her from the earliest possible age.
3. Give your child the gift of high expectations, and create a positive and motivating environment to foster your child's school success.
4. Keep your child accountable for her schoolwork so she thrives in school. Stay actively involved in your child's educational process by participating in academic and extracurricular activities whenever possible.
5. Keep life and learning exciting by providing stimulating experiences to supplement and reinforce your child's intellectual growth through physical and social activity.
6. Address any personal special needs or challenges and remove any distractions to your child's intellectual growth so that your child can maximize her capacity to learn.
7. Help your child focus mentally by removing from her life excessive physical, emotional, and social distractions to the learning process. This may mean seeking professional assistance if your child's needs indicate that is necessary.

"Train up a child in the way he should go, Even when he is old he will not depart from it" (Proverbs 22:6).

Do your best to give your child the encouragement, education, and resources she needs to be successful in her academic and intellectual pursuits.

7

THE INSTRUCTION MANUAL

The Role of Scripture in Your Parenting

"Dr. Jones, I have a seven-year-old son who won't eat his food. He also throws temper tantrums when he doesn't get his way. What should I do?"

Or what about this question? "Dr. Smith, my twelve-year-old won't go to bed at night. And when I correct her she curses at me. Please help!"

Although the names are fictitious, dialogues like this fill the airwaves across our country every day. Parents are desperately seeking answers to the complex challenges of parenting. In some cases, they will listen to anyone who can get a spot on a broadcast.

THE SCRIPTURES: THE ULTIMATE AUTHORITY FOR YOUR PARENTING

There are plenty of voices responding to the cries for help. The question is, Do these voices have real answers that parents can depend on? Some do and some don't. There are some very good counselors giving very solid advice. To whom should you listen? How do you know if their counsel is solid?

There is only one place where advice transcends color, culture, or class. Harry Shields and Gary Bredfelt made a very clear statement about biblical authority in their book *Caring for Souls:*

> In many regards, when we speak of the Bible as our authority for matters of faith and practice, we mean the Bible serves as a kind of map. In the same way that a map gives direction and provides a point of reference for the traveler in making judgements and decisions, so also does the written Word of God for the Christian pilgrim on his journey. A map is not the only source of information a traveler employs. Along the way are many travelers' aids and information centers. People seek to give direction. Some fellow travelers have already traversed the land and seek to offer guidance to the pilgrim. And, of course, the traveler can make his own observations. Each traveler, through the use of the senses and reasoning skills, can make judgements about the direction to proceed. By study not just of maps but of the terrain, the direction of the sun, or the position of the stars in the night sky, the traveler can make reasonable assertions about the direction his journey should take.
>
> The wise traveler knows that the map offers the greatest authority for the journey. He trusts it. It alone serves as the standard by which he can judge the accuracy of his observations or the quality of the directions or advice from fellow travelers. It alone can serve as the ultimate authority for deciding which way is the true way to the planned destination. In much the same manner, the Bible serves as our map through this dark world. It judges the opinions and "truths" of men. By it we gain the essential information about God and godly living that we could know through no other means. And it is that information that rightly orders all of life. It is the information that comes from God as a special revelation that unlocks the truths found in the natural revelation of God. It is the Word, rightly interpreted, that enables us to fashion a view of the world consistent with the nature and will of our Maker.[1]

That extended quote is one of the clearest statements I have ever read about biblical authority. It should motivate every parent to a serious consideration of the Bible.

Use the Bible as your ultimate source of authority for parenting. "All Scripture is inspired by God and profitable for teaching, for reproof, for correction, for training in righteousness; so that the man of God may be adequate, equipped for every good work" (2 Timothy 3:16–17).

You have the opportunity in your parental practices to allow the Scriptures to be your guide. The Bible can help you with the information you need to teach your children, and it can show you how to respond to problems in your home.

It is all right to listen to counselors if you evaluate and validate their counsel based on how it conforms to the clear teaching of God's Word. But that assumes that you spend enough time in the Scriptures to recognize whether the counselor is basing his ideas on Scripture.

The uniqueness of the Bible

This quote taken from a doctoral dissertation project I completed gives a snapshot of why I believe the Bible should have a unique place as the authority for your parenting.

> There is no better place to start in a search for parenting insight than the perennial best-seller: the Bible. Its advice comes from writers who come from a variety of nations, ethnic groups, economic strata, educational levels, and life situations. A look at some of the observations made by McDowell (1972) gives a compelling description of its uniqueness.
>
> Here is a book:
> Written over a 1600-year span.
> Written over 60 generations.
> Written by 40 plus authors from every walk of life including kings, peasants, philosophers, fishermen, poets, statesmen, scholars, etc.
> Written in different places.
> Written at different times.
> Written during different moods.
> Written in three languages.[2]
>
> The Bible has been translated and retranslated more than any other book in existence. The Bible is a book that offers divinely inspired insights for parents of all classes, cultures, and life situations.

Therefore, it is uniquely qualified to address the parenting questions for all people, including yours.

Distinguish between authoritative and illustrative ideas

Ideas that are based on the Scripture and illustrate biblical truth can probably be helpful to you if they are properly applied. But even though an idea is based on the Scripture, it may not be authoritative. The idea may simply offer you insights that illustrate what the Scripture is teaching. Evaluate the idea carefully to see if it rises to the level of a command. If it does, obey it. If it does not rise to the level of a universal command, pray for wisdom from God about how you should apply the teaching to your particular situation.

A good example would be the numerous passages of Scripture that refer to spanking as a method used to correct misbehavior. It the clear teaching of Scripture that in some instances spanking is an acceptable method of responding to childhood misbehavior. But it would be incorrect to accept teaching that says spanking should be used in every instance that a child misbehaves.

A parallel to the teaching about parental spanking would be the clear teaching of Scripture that God chastises us sometimes for our sin. But it is also true that most of the time we experience God's grace rather than His punishment. In most cases, He lovingly corrects us and redirects our behavior when we fail to live up to His standards.

That way of dealing with us is more difficult and time consuming, but God takes the time to give us what we need to grow. God's punishment is always balanced with His love. In the same way, a parent always has to balance the passages of Scripture that counsel corrective discipline with the passages that challenge parents to stay sensitive to the emotional and physical needs of their children at all times.

I believe the Bible teaches that sometimes spanking is an appropriate response to a child's rebellion. However, I believe that spanking is often an easy but inappropriate way to respond to most misbehavior. Unfortunately, those who offer it as the standard method take the biblical references they cite as universal commands rather than principles to be carefully applied based on the needs of the child. This is an example of mistaking a passage of Scripture that is illustrative for one that is mandatory for all situations. Avoid that kind of thinking and counsel.

Recognize the limitations of human experience

"This is how my friend did it. So I am going to do the same thing." That may not be a good idea. Set limits on how much you rely on the experience of others for your parenting insights. Paul reminds us of this in the epistle to the Colossians. "See to it that no one takes you captive through hollow and deceptive philosophy, which depends on human tradition and the basic principles of this world rather than on Christ" (Colossians 2:8 NIV).

If your friend made choices in accordance with Scripture, then you can copy his methods. If not, you should think very carefully about basing your parenting decisions on his example.

Every child is different and deserves to have his needs responded to as an individual. You cannot always assume what works for one child will be appropriate for another.

Listen to human reason offered by parents, friends, and counselors. But don't let their counsel rise to the level of biblical authority if it is not based on the clear teaching of Scripture.

Don't get snagged by the "lifestyles of the rich and famous"

Avoid using the insights from the rich and famous as your ultimate source of authority. In our society we have a tendency to give universal credibility to people if they are successful in the entertainment or athletic worlds. Be careful about accepting the counsel of the rich and famous.

The Scripture teaches that those who leave God out of their parenting philosophy are not good models to follow, even if they have lots of money and resources. There is a clear warning in the Bible to avoid following the example of the world. "I urge you, as aliens and strangers in the world, to abstain from sinful desires, which war against your soul" (1 Peter 2:11 NIV).

Don't listen to the standards of false religions

Filter out the truth statements about parental authority from false statements that go against the Scriptures. Filter out the truth statements that come from sources of authority that go against the Scripture to guide parental authority. Be careful to avoid listening to the wrong voices. There are a lot of people who promote good moral advice. It is OK to heed that good moral advice if it reflects sensitivity to the clear teaching of Scripture.

On the other hand, if that advice appears to contradict what the Bible says about parenting and interpersonal relationships, then you have to be very careful. You should always accept an appropriate interpretation of the Scripture in the area it addresses over the opinion of another religious position if you are trying to base your parenting practice on the Bible's teaching.

Here is where you have to be careful. Not every presentation of "God's" methods are consistent with the accurate teaching of Scripture. If you are in doubt, consult with your pastor or someone else who has a sound grasp of how to properly interpret the Scripture.

Human reason can't solve all the problems

God has given you a strong mind. You should carefully use "informed judgment" to respond to the daily opportunities you have to disciple your child. There is a key word in that previous sentence—the word *informed.* The Bible warns us not to rely exclusively on our own judgment when it is not informed by the Scriptures. The prophet Ezekiel cautioned against relying on human rumination. "Son of man, prophesy against the prophets of Israel who are now prophesying. Say to those who prophesy out of their own imagination: 'Hear the word of the Lord!'" (Ezekiel 13:2 NIV).

God's insights and ideas can give you the foundation you need to effectively develop your child. Then you will have a "sanctified" judgment that God can use in a powerful way. That raises a natural question. How do your keep your own judgment in proper perspective?

Let the Bible be your searchlight and your spotlight

As you plan to develop your children, the Bible will be a useful resource and tool. Sometimes you will be searching for direction for the future; the Bible can help you. In other cases, you will need immediate insight. The Bible can help you there, too. The psalmist recognized that when he described God's Word. "Your word is a lamp to my feet and a light to my path" (Psalm 119:105).

A particular verse of Scripture that points parents in the way they should develop their children and provides a searchlight for illumination is Proverbs 22:6. "Train up a child in the way he should go, even when he is old he will not depart from it." This verse gives parents an important reference point for the way they should help their children achieve God's perfect plan for their lives.

Another scriptural reference that may help you in a difficult moment is Proverbs 15:1. "A gentle answer turns away wrath, but a harsh word stirs up anger." This verse could prevent an abusive statement being made to a child and will give you the wisdom you need to avoid worsening a challenging situation with your child and stirring up further anger.

There are many other passages of Scripture that can give you the direction you need to shape the character of your children and make daily parenting decisions. Becoming a serious student of Scripture will give you the practical wisdom that will make you much more effective as a parent. That raises the question of how the Bible can help you with equipping your child to function successfully in his world.

Adopt the Bible as your main character curriculum

Teach your children scriptural principles of character development and the themes that are on the heart of God. I remember an experience I had during my undergraduate college years that illustrated the heart of a young man who had not been taught the worth and dignity of every person. Although it happened more than twenty-six years ago, I will never forget that day as a freshman when I was walking across my university campus. As I approached a bus that took students across the campus, the window of the bus came down, and almost simultaneously, I felt the full force of that young man's saliva as he propelled it on my face and the words he shouted so my ears could hear them. The words "Nigger! Nigger!" spoken more than twenty-six years ago still resonate in my ears almost like it was yesterday.

Either he was a slow learner or his parents had not taught him to respect people who were different from him. Not only was that poor manners, it violated the Bible's picture of who I was. Galatians 3 makes it clear that my identity is not defined by ethnicity or gender, but my relationship with God through Christ. "There is neither Jew nor Greek, there is neither slave nor free man, there is neither male nor female; for you are all one in Christ Jesus" (Galatians 3:28).

This verse clearly teaches that diversity is a commentary on the creative majesty of God. Diversity is a gift to be enjoyed, not endured. It is a powerful reality to be celebrated, not condemned. Placing this conviction on the heart of your child will help him display a powerful witness to a world in desperate need to embrace that truth.

If you use the Bible as your main character curriculum, it will touch every aspect of your child's life. The Bible will help you prepare your children to walk with God, have healthy interpersonal relationships, and relate to other people they come in contact with in a way that honors God. Although there are many places where your child can receive biblical instruction, such as your church, you have a unique opportunity to be the primary teacher for your child. As you carry out this role, avoid the extremes and include a broad overview of the themes that are on the heart of God.

I have listed a few examples of those themes below. One reason you have such an important role in the lives of your children is that you can both communicate and illustrate the power of these principles by the way you live your life on a daily basis. Don't underestimate your role as a communicator and illustrator of biblical truth for your children.

1. The worth of the individual (Genesis 1:27)
2. The sanctity of life (Genesis 9:6)
3. Protection of personal property (Exodus 22:7)
4. Benevolence for the disadvantaged (Exodus 22:25–27)
5. Protection for the poor (Exodus 22:21–24)
6. Sensitivity for the physically challenged (Leviticus 19:14)
7. Impartial administration of justice (Deuteronomy 1:16–17)
8. Advocacy for the voiceless (Proverbs 31:8–9)
9. Punishment of evildoers (Romans 13:1–4)
10. Respect for all people and races (Acts 10:34)
11. Preservation of the family (Ephesians 5:18–6:4)
12. Provision for the widows and orphans (James 1:27)

All these areas are important to God. If you take the Bible seriously as the authority for your life, they should be an important part of the values you teach your children.

Develop a sound understanding of Scripture

All Scripture does not have the same degree of relevance and application to the issues you will face as a parent. However, all Scripture that addresses the challenges of parenting has God's full authority and provides a viable approach to your responsibility. In order to get the greatest possible benefit from parenting according to Scripture, it will be helpful if you understand a number of categories of biblical truths.

1. **Precepts**—Clearly defined standards that God expects each believer to observe as an expression of commitment to Him (examples: Deuteronomy 6:4–9; 2 Corinthians 6:14–16).
2. **Promises**—Assurances made by God to the believer based on the authority of His Word and the strength of His character (example: 1 John 1:9).
3. **Practice**—Ethical teaching given to the believer as a standard for addressing situations that arise in the believer's life experience (example: Ephesians 6:4).
4. **Patterns**—Examples of responses given by God in Scripture for the believer to prevent repetition of acts of rebellion against and resistance to God's standard for the believer (example: 1 Corinthians 10:6–11).
5. **Principles**—Truths and moral axioms given to guide the directions and routines of our life experiences (example: Proverbs 22:6).
6. **Program**—A clear description of God's intentions and eternal plan for the individual believer, the family, the church, the nation of Israel, and the world as presented in the Scripture (example: Ephesians 5:21–6:4).

Use the Bible as a reference tool for counseling your child

The Bible can give you insight for some of the challenges you face on a daily basis. You will find practical help by examining some of the principles outlined in the Scripture. Encouraging your children to memorize passages of Scripture that give helpful insights for their lives will help them lay a foundation they will thank you for when they reach maturity. I have listed a few examples.

Self-control—"Cease from anger and forsake wrath; do not fret; it leads only to evildoing" (Psalm 37:8).

Value of hard work—"Poor is he who works with a negligent hand, but the hand of the diligent makes rich. He who gathers in summer is a son who acts wisely, but he who sleeps in harvest is a son who acts shamefully" (Proverbs 10:4–5).

De-escalating conflict—"A gentle answer turns away wrath, but a harsh word stirs up anger" (Proverbs 15:1).

Danger of pride—"Pride goes before destruction, and a haughty spirit before stumbling. It is better to be humble in spirit with the lowly than to divide the spoil with the proud" (Proverbs 16:18–19).

Importance of companionship—"Two are better than one because they have a good return for their labor. For if either of them falls, the one will lift up his companion. But woe to the one who falls when there is not one to lift him up" (Ecclesiastes 4:9–10).

Consideration of others—"In everything, therefore, treat people the same way you want them to treat you, for this is the Law and the Prophets" (Matthew 7:12).

Impact of peer association—"Do not be deceived: 'Bad company corrupts good morals'" (1 Corinthians 15:33).

Perseverance—"Let us not lose heart in doing good, for in due time we will reap if we do not grow weary" (Galatians 6:9).

Not holding grudges—"Be angry, and yet do not sin; do not let the sun go down on your anger, and do not give the devil an opportunity" (Ephesians 4:26–27).

Importance of attitude—"Finally, brethren, whatever is true, whatever is honorable, whatever is right, whatever is pure, whatever is lovely, whatever is of good repute, if there is any excellence and if anything worthy of praise, dwell on these things" (Philippians 4:8).

Importance of self-discipline—"For God has not given us a spirit of timidity, but of power and love and discipline" (2 Timothy 1:7).

Value of compassion—"To sum up, all of you be harmonious, sympathetic, brotherly, kindhearted, and humble in spirit; not returning evil for evil or insult for insult, but giving a blessing instead; for you were called for this very purpose that you might inherit a blessing" (1 Peter 3:8–9).

This list of passages is just a sampling of the kind of help you can receive from the Scripture for addressing the daily issues and challenges you face.

Build a biblical filter for making family decisions

Make your decisions based on the clear teaching of Scripture and help your children learn how to apply that practice to their lives. If you develop biblical literacy, the Bible will give you an excellent filter for evaluating ideas and information presented by others to help you with your parenting. The Scripture, unlike any other material you will read, is absolutely pure. The words of the psalmist give a beautiful picture of that reality.

> The law of the Lord is perfect, restoring the soul;
> The testimony of the Lord is sure, making wise the simple.
> The precepts of the Lord are right, rejoicing the heart;
> The commandment of the Lord is pure, enlightening the eyes.
> The fear of the Lord is clean, enduring forever;
> The judgments of the Lord are true; they are righteous altogether.
> They are more desirable than gold, yes, than much fine gold;
> Sweeter also than honey and the drippings of the honeycomb.
> Morever, by them Your servant is warned;
> In keeping them there is great reward.
>
> —Psalm 19:7–11

As you evaluate information that gives you counsel about parenting, there is no better source for making good decisions than the Bible.

Provide age-level tools and resources for your child

One of the ways you can help your child develop more respect for the Bible is to provide resources and tools that will help him learn and grow in his level of knowledge. I strongly recommend that you make sure your child has these resources at his age and grade level:

- Bible
- Bible dictionary
- Bible background materials
- Encyclopedia

If you make these resources available in your home, it will increase the likelihood of your child's having the exposure he needs to learn to respect the importance of the Bible.

THE SCRIPTURES HAVE POWER WHEN PROPERLY USED

You have to apply the Scripture to your parenting challenges and opportunities expectantly and correctly to experience the power of God's truth. M. R. DeHann tells an interesting story about a Christian who saw the power of God through applying the truths of Scripture. I hope you find great encouragement in this story in the same way I did.

> A Christian in the line of duty was once called upon to visit a man in an asylum who had severe mental hallucinations. Recalling the story in I Samuel 16, how David had calmed Saul in his demented moments by singing one of his precious, inspired songs to him, and conscious too of the power of the Bible upon his own soul, he decided to read from the Psalms to this one who was mentally tormented. He found that the Word of God had a soothing and "healing " effect on the poor fellow. He therefore returned many times to the asylum to perform this spiritual labor of love—almost invariably with happy results. One day the superintendent, an unconverted man,

said, "Your treatment may be good, but it does not always succeed." "What makes you say that?" asked the Christian. "Well," said the other, "in desperation last night I tried to calm the patient by your method, when he was in one of his perturbed and frantic moods, and my efforts failed completely." The Christian was surprised. " What portion did you read to him?" he asked. "Oh, I just began at the front—all about a most high and mighty prince named James . . . !" Apparently in his ignorance the attendant had read the preface to the King James Bible, which of course was not inspired. No wonder it had no effect! Only the life-giving Word of God has attached to it the immutable promise: "It shall not return unto me void, but it shall accomplish that which I please" (Isa. 55:11). No one can read the Scripture and remain unmoved! The Bible's influence cannot be shaken off. Every time it comes in contact with us it either increases our doom or draws us graciously toward Heaven!

Take the time to learn how to properly interpret the Bible and apply it appropriately to your parenting challenges and God will give you wisdom and insight.

FAITH STEPS

1. Place the Bible in the position of authority over your life.

2. Teach your child the Bible as a regular part of the family routine.

3. Establish a regular Bible reading program as a part of the family routine.

4. Give your child a broad understanding of the major themes of Scripture.

5. Provide tools and resources to help your child grow in his understanding of the Bible.

A PARENT'S PRAYER

Father, Thank You for giving us the Bible to help guide me as a parent. Help me learn the Bible so I can teach it to my children. Help me learn to place Your truth above popular ideas. Guide me to the Scriptures so that I will make decisions honorable to You. Give me the courage to make Your Word my source of authority as I lead my children and help them reach personal maturity. Amen.

PARENTING INSIGHTS

SPECIAL CARE INSTRUCTIONS

Research Highlight: Your Child's View of the Bible

George Barna's recent surveys related to the Bible yielded the following findings in a summarized form.[3]

- The percentage of people who read their Bibles on a weekly basis rose from 34 percent in 1996 to 40 percent in 2000.
- More than 60 percent all American adults agree that the Bible is totally accurate in all of its teachings.
- A little less than half the American population believes that the Bible is absolutely accurate and that everything in it can be taken literally.
- Interestingly, although millions of Americans believe the Bible is accurate in all of its teachings, a significant number of those people do not relate the relevance of Scripture to their everyday lives by seeking to read and apply the Bible. For every five adults who were asked about the relevance of the Ten Commandments only one thought it was relevant for today.
- Some 92 percent of American households own at least one copy of the Christian Bible.
- Most adults (56 percent) believe the most important proclamation the Bible makes is taking care of our families.
- The people who responded to surveys and made a claim that they were Bible readers spent an average of fifty-two minutes per week reading the Bible.

RESEARCH APPLICATIONS

If you are the average parent, there are several actions you may want to take to make the Scripture have a more significant impact on your personal life and the life of your child.

1. Commit to reading your Bible on a daily basis and encourage your children to follow your example.
2. Search the Scriptures daily for principles relevant to your parenting responsibilities.
3. Accept the authority of the Bible over your contemporary parenting challenges and responsibilities.
4. Give your child a personal copy of the Bible.
5. Develop a sound enough understanding of the Bible that you can explain and defend its authority and relevance to your children.
6. Give your children a broad understanding of the history, structure, and content of the Bible.
7. Make it a habit to consult the Bible when you are making important decisions so that your children recognize the relevance of the Scripture to your everyday life decisions.

"All Scripture is inspired by God and profitable for teaching, for reproof, for correction, for training in righteousness" (1 Timothy 3:16).

Help your child develop a high level of competence in using his Bible and confidence in its relevance to his life.

8

SPECIAL DELIVERY

The Importance of a Godly Mother

Franklin Graham has a fascinating life story. Instead of the scripted experience one would expect from the son of a man loved and admired by Christians around the world, he came to God in his own way. Really, that's how we all come to God. But his story has special intrigue just because he is the son of Billy Graham.

If one were to examine Franklin Graham's pilgrimage to God it would be apparent that lots of people were used by God to impact the life of this servant of God. But you would be hard-put to find anyone who had more impact than his mother, Ruth Bell Graham. From her tireless discipline, sympathetic spirit, and consistent presentation of spiritual truth was forged a set of impressions that God ultimately used to help Franklin find his way to the cross of Christ.

Franklin's own words in his book *Rebel with a Cause* give us a glimpse into the impact his mother had on the family.

> Mama was always a great example to children in every way. One was by having a good attitude about Daddy's long trips. She longed for her husband when he was away, and she knew that we missed him too. But she was determined to make the best of it.
>
> When it came time for Daddy to leave again, it was Mama's lightheartedness that held us together as a family. She didn't complain. "He'll be back in a month," she would say matter-of-factly.
>
> If the washing machine broke down or there were other problems while he was away—and often there were—Mama handled them herself. And that would be the end of it.
>
> But perhaps the most wonderful gift she gave us related to Daddy's trips was that she never threatened us with "Wait till your father comes home. I'll let him handle this." She was wise and knew that if she resorted to that tactic, we would always live in dread of his return.
>
> It may sound trite, but it's true: Without my mother's faithful, dependable, strong presence in the home front, my father's world-wide preaching of the gospel of Jesus Christ to millions might never have been possible.[1]

Wow! What a legacy of faithfulness! I have always held Billy Graham in high regard, with deep respect for his life and ministry. I still do. After reading Franklin Graham's autobiography, though, I have a deep respect as well for Ruth Bell Graham. Her story is the story of untold mothers who have made a commitment to providing love and nurture to millions of children. They do that because in their hearts they believe their children are a special delivery from God to them.

Hannah had that kind of conviction. She offers an incredible picture of how God places in the hand of a mother the potential to shape the life of a person God has created and given a special mission and purpose.

ANCHORED BY A LIFE OF FAITH AND A COMMITMENT TO PRAYER

Hannah was passionate about her relationship with God and her desire to be a mother.

> Then Hannah rose after eating and drinking in Shiloh. Now Eli the priest was sitting on the seat by the doorpost of the temple of the Lord. She, greatly

> distressed, prayed to the Lord and wept bitterly. She made a vow and said, "O Lord of hosts, if You will indeed look on the affliction of Your maidservant and remember me, and not forget Your maidservant, but will give Your maidservant a son, then I will give him to the Lord all the days of his life, and a razor shall not come on his head." (1 Samuel 1:9–11)

A godly mother has to have a passion for her role and opportunity to care for her child. Your child's growth will be boosted tremendously by a mother who is deeply convinced that her child has been provided to her as a gift from God.

Most mothers have been given a wonderful maternal instinct that causes them to display almost miraculous selflessness on behalf of their children. My mother, Helen Mercer, is a tremendous example of this selflessness. Honestly, I believe if it is possible to be too committed to your children, she fits into that category. But I am so thankful to God for a mother who always challenged us to perform beyond our circumstances. I remember many instances during my years of growth and development when she deprived herself of what many would call the basic necessities of life so that her children could have extras.

She epitomizes a mother who has a tireless commitment to her children. My mind and heart have the indelible imprint of her prayers of quiet desperation to God for provision for the family's needs. She has always had an overcoming faith that God used early in my life to inspire and motivate me.

The reason I am writing this book today is that even when we didn't have much materially as a family, my mother always told us we could achieve whatever we dreamed of. Once she told us that all her energies and efforts were expended to help our dreams become realities.

Unfortunately, a few mothers see their responsibilities as a burden rather than a blessing. If a mother sees her children as a burden, the home will not be the priority for her life or ministry. But that is not what a child needs, nor what God blesses.

Commit yourself to make sure you have released your children to God. When you wake up each day remind yourself, *My child belongs to God.* This will keep your perspective in line with Scripture and reduce your stress level.

DEDICATED TO THE FAMILY AS A MINISTRY PRIORITY

In the book of Titus, Paul challenged older and younger women to place their families as a high personal priority. This passage of Scripture could create much distress for a young mother if she misunderstands it. The passage does not teach that the only role a mother has is in the home, but it does teach that the home should be one of a mother's highest personal priorities.

> Older women likewise are to be reverent in their behavior, not malicious gossips nor enslaved to much wine, teaching what is good, so that they may encourage the young women to love their husbands, to love their children, to be sensible, pure, workers at home, kind, being subject to their own husbands, so that the word of God will not be dishonored. (Titus 2:3–5)

The home cannot be minimized in the life of a godly mother. I know of no better example of a mother who has made her home the highest priority of her life than my wife, Annie Mercer. Since the birth of our first child she has placed all personal ambitions on hold to make sure the needs of the household are met. For more than twenty years, her role as a mother has been the primary passion of her life. I am so thankful to God that Annie has a servant spirit so that my children have had the best care children could possibly get from an earthly mother. She is the most resourceful and creative woman I know.

My youngest daughter did a pretty good job of describing her mother when she had to complete an assignment at school answering the question "My Mom Is Special Because . . ."

MY MOM IS SPECIAL BECAUSE

She is very pretty and *a very good cook and substitute teacher.*
I like it when my mom *takes me to places like Six Flags when the rest of the family can't come.*
My mom can do many things! I think she is best at *cooking and smiling.*

My mom has a pretty smile. I like to make her smile by *doing funny things.*
My mom is as pretty as *the rosebush we have at home.*
My mom is smart. *She even knows what to do when you measure a piece of material.*

God did not require her—and neither did I—to choose to give up her own career that may have taken her away from our home while the kids were growing up. In the case of God's call on Annie Mercer's life, she sensed that it was for an almost absolute focus on the needs and challenges of being a mother. She responded with total obedience. Annie's focus on the home has allowed her to be at home when the children finished their school classes and at the school when the kids had special activities and programs.

Listen to the voice of God to know exactly what God's call for your role as a mother is. Each mother has to hear God's call in terms of exactly how she fulfills God's call to the role of mother. Don't let anyone else put you on a guilt trip that is not based on the clear teaching of Scripture. But do obey the clear teaching of Scripture and God's leading for your life as a mother. Check your own heart by asking yourself a simple question: At this time in my life and in the growth and development of my children, how do I best fulfill God's purpose in my role as mother? Once you get the answer to that question, you can make the decision God places on your heart.

TRANSMITS FAITH TO HER CHILDREN

Not only must a godly mother make family a priority, she must also seize the opportunity to give her children a spiritual legacy. In 2 Timothy 1:5, Paul speaks of the privilege Timothy had of having a mother and grandmother who shared their spiritual values with him: "For I am mindful of the sincere faith within you, which first dwelt in your grandmother Lois and your mother Eunice, and I am sure that it is in you as well."

For all of their lives, my children have had the privilege of having a mother who has been a part of a daily prayer time. And when ministry has taken me out of town, Annie has guided our children through a daily period of committing their days and hearts to the Lord through a regular prayer time.

Transmitting faith to children sometimes means capturing the informal and formal moments of life and using those as opportunities to teach children important personal values. A dear friend of our family, Marilyn Skemp, related a personal story about how her mother not only impacted her children's lives but generations to come through her sensitivity to converting a childish spirit into a teachable moment. Marilyn's description of this experience is powerful and instructive for other mothers.

Marilyn watched her grandfather model a deep commitment to personal prayer. From early childhood to adulthood, she watched him express a simple, heartfelt prayer at every meal at large family gatherings. "Kind Father, accept our thanks for these blessings; pardon and forgive our sins, we ask in Christ's name. Amen."

Marilyn and her brother always had a deep love and respect for their grandfather and learned a lot from his example. But it was during a playful moment that she learned a lesson she would never forget. One day she and her brother were mimicking the slow southern drawl which her grandfather seemed to use only when he prayed this particular prayer.

When Marilyn's mother saw what she and her brother were doing, she captured the moment. "Our mother quietly and gently said to us, 'Do you know why your grandfather says that prayer?' Then she told us about his father praying the same prayer at every family dinner and how she had grown up hearing the same words prayed in the same manner."

Marilyn was forever changed by that moment of instruction from her mother. "I must admit from that point forward the prayer had new meaning and did give me comfort. On the few occasions when my grandfather would change the prayer he always got my attention."

The most powerful impact of that moment did not show during Marilyn's teenage years; it came about when she was an adult and had children of her own to teach and nurture.

> My grandfather died in February a week after his ninetieth birthday. The next holiday was Easter. The whole family was seated to eat lunch, and it was decided I would give the blessing. I prayed his prayer with reverence, in the manner he would have prayed it.
>
> When the prayer was complete there was silence, and my grandmother said, "Thank you." We now pray his prayer at all the major holiday family meals.

> It is a way to include my grandfather in the family meal. It is also something I want my children to learn and know. The prayer is a part of our family legacy.

This legacy of prayer now has a special meaning for three generations because a mother converted an informal moment into a special teaching opportunity.

Mothers usually spend more time with children in informal times and because of this have a special opportunity to capture a spontaneous moment and teach their children some special lessons about faith and life. Ask God to give you special sensitivity to special opportunities that arise during the course of a day. Your natural inclination will be to let frustration crowd out the chances to convert daily life encounters into teachable moments. Resist that temptation.

IS SKILLFUL IN PROVIDING FOR PRACTICAL FAMILY NEEDS

The Bible points out that mothers have a unique opportunity to impact children spiritually. The classic passage of Scripture on the excellent wife, Proverbs 31:10–31, illustrates that there is no domain of life that a mother's life does not touch.

> An excellent wife, who can find?
> For her worth is far above jewels.
> The heart of her husband trusts in her,
> And he will have lack of gain.
> She does him good and not evil
> All the days of her life.
> She looks for wool and flax
> And works with her hands in delight.
> She is like merchant ships;
> She brings her food from afar.
> She rises also while it is still night
> And gives food to her household
> And portions to her maidens.
> She considers a field and buys it;

From her earnings she plants a vineyard.
She girds herself with strength
And makes her arms strong.
She senses that her gain is good;
Her lamp does not go out at night.
She stretches out her hands to the distaff,
And her hands grasp the spindle.
She extends her hand to the poor,
And she stretches out her hands to the needy.
She is not afraid of snow for her household,
For all her household are clothed with scarlet.
She makes coverings for herself;
Her clothing is fine linen and purple.
Her husband is known in the gates,
When he sits among the elders of the land.
She makes linen garments and sells them,
And supplies belts to the tradesmen.
Strength and dignity are her clothing,
And she smiles at the future.
She opens her mouth in wisdom,
And the teaching of kindness is on her tongue.
She looks well to the ways of her household,
And does not eat the bread of idleness.
Her children rise up and bless her;
Her husband also, and he praises her, saying:
"Many daughters have done nobly,
But you excel them all."
Charm is deceitful and beauty is vain,
But a woman who fears the Lord, she shall be praised.
Give her the product of her hands,
And let her works praise her in the gates.

TAKES CARE OF HERSELF SO THAT SHE CAN BE STRONG ENOUGH TO SUPPORT HER FAMILY

A striking feature of the life of the woman described in Proverbs 31 is that even as she cared for others she still took time to take care of her own physical, emotional, and spiritual needs. Notice verse 13, "She looks for wool and flax and works with her hands in delight"; verse 17, "She girds herself with strength"; verse 22, "She makes coverings for herself"; and verse 25, "Strength and dignity are her clothing, and she smiles at the future."

Just as you should consider imitating the Proverbs 31 woman's capacity as a wife and mother, so it would be wise to learn from her personal care practices. It is a fundamental principle of life that we can only give to others if we are strong ourselves.

Almost every week during the last year I have fastened airplane seat belts and heard a repeated announcement from the flight attendant as they give instructions just prior to takeoff. "If you are traveling with an older person, a young child, or someone who needs assistance, first, put the oxygen mask on yourself and then place the mask on the person traveling with you." Seems selfish, doesn't it? But it is not.

It is fundamental to your personal health and success as a mother. You have to create time in your personal routine to take care of your own spiritual, emotional, social, and physical needs if you are going to be a strong mother.

Don't let Proverbs 31 intimidate you. Instead, let it inspire you. Just try to embark on a journey of strengthening your personal and spiritual life one step at a time. Mimicking the character of the woman described in Proverbs 31 may be a lifelong journey, but it is worth striving for.

IS IN A POSITION OF HONOR AND DISTINCTION

Jesus made a reference to His mother that should be instructive to us all. During the last phase of Jesus' ministry on the earth, He recognized His mother and made provision for her care and well-being. "When Jesus then saw His mother, and the disciple whom He loved standing nearby, He said to His mother, 'Woman, behold, your son!' Then He said to the disciple, 'Behold, your mother!' From that hour the disciple took her into his own household" (John 19:26–27).

It was no accident that during Jesus' last days on this earth a primary concern for Him was that His mother was taken care of. I believe this passage is in the Scriptures to give us a window into the heart of our Lord and motivate us to follow in His steps.

We also can learn a great deal from Susannah Wesley's response to a letter from her son Samuel. He once began a letter to her with "Madame." She wrote back, "Sammy, I do not love distance or ceremony. There is more love and tenderness in the name of mother than in all the complimental titles in the world."

Mothers should be honored. This is especially true in a culture that sometimes devalues the role of motherhood. Mothers should expect respect from their children. This is something that will not only strengthen a mother's relationship with her child, but will also improve the child's quality of life. "Honor your father and your mother, that your days may be prolonged in the land which the Lord your God gives you" (Exodus 20:12).

Insist on your child's showing you respect. If he fails to respect you, make sure he experiences the kinds of consequences that will decrease future incidents of disrespect. Also find ways to reward your child when he consistently demonstrates respect for you. That will reinforce this behavior. The term *mother* deserves the highest level of affection and honor.

Lindsey O' Connor wrote a sketch of Susannah Wesley that gives every committed mother a model of dedication and commitment to her children worth imitating.

> Her name was Susannah Wesley, the mother of John and Charles Wesley. This intelligent 17th-century woman bore 19 children and demonstrated discipline in her routine, child training, and devotions, in which she spent two hours each day. She held on to her faith despite a hard life.
>
> Susannah suffered from ill heath and a difficult marriage. She faced poverty, two house fires and the deaths of nine of her children. No wonder she struggled with depression. And Susannah lived as a "married single mom." Susannah's husband left frequently for long stretches of time, including debtors' prison followed by seven winters away doing church work. She cared for her 10 surviving children alone, and her hard work produced fruit. John wrote 42,000 sermons and 233 books, and Charles wrote more than 8,000 hymns. The brothers became the co-founders of Methodism and leaders of the evangelical revival of the Church of England. Describing his mother's influence, John said, "I learned more about Christianity from my mother than all the theologians of England."[2]

This is a mother who deserves honor and praise.

Faith Steps

1. Build a strong platform of personal convictions as a mother and use it well.

2. Take care of yourself so that you will have the capacity to care for your family.

3. Commit yourself to enjoy your role as mother.

4. Create a standard of respectability and insist on respect from your children.

5. If God gives you a career, enjoy it; if He does not, enjoy investing your life in your children.

A Parent's Prayer

Father, Please give my child a mother who recognizes her uniqueness. Help me see the position of mother as the most strategic role on earth. Give me the passion to make my child my highest earthly priority. Help me to live up to the position of honor You have called me to as a mother. Amen.

PARENTING INSIGHTS

SPECIAL CARE INSTRUCTIONS

Research Highlight: A Mother's Nurture

The research about the central role a mother can play in the growth and development of a child is astounding.[3]

RESEARCH HIGHLIGHTS

- God gives a mother the incredible capacity to provide the complete needs a child has for emotional and physical sustenance for nine months of gestation in utero.
- A mother's diet during the period of her pregnancy can influence her child's health for her entire life.
- Toxic substances in the mother's body have the potential to be transmitted to the baby in her womb and cause lifelong health problems for her child.
- Excessive stress in the mother's life can create problems for the baby in her womb.
- At birth a child can distinguish her mother's smell from anyone else's.
- After a child has been in the world for ninety-six hours she can distinguish her mother's voice from anyone else's.
- A newborn baby prefers the sound of her mother's voice over that of her father or of any other woman.
- A mother's breast milk after birth has the capacity to supply all of a child's nutritional needs for her first six months of life outside the womb.

These research results point to implications for parenting behavior that don't require an incredible amount of money, but a high level of commitment.

RESEARCH APPLICATIONS

1. A mother should eat a healthy and nutritious diet while she is pregnant with her child.

2. Each mother should try to eliminate every toxic substance she possibly can from her body while she is carrying her child in the womb.

3. A mother can decrease the negative impact of stress on the growth of her child by intentionally reducing it in her life.

4. Every mother should attempt to spend as much time as possible with her child when she is first born into the world.

5. A mother should seriously consider the benefits of breast-feeding her child for her first months of life.

6. Every mother should seek to give her child as much opportunity to bond and attach to her as possible during the critical early months of the child's life.

7. Every mother should enjoy the powerful position of influence she has on her child's life.

"Behold, children are a gift of the Lord, the fruit of the womb is a reward" (Psalm 127:3).

9

GOD'S SECURITY SYSTEM

The Father's Influence on a Child's Life

"Dad is destiny"

"Rich or poor, black or white, young or old . . . the single most important factor determining the success or failure of a child is the presence or absence of a biological father in the home."[1] Those words from a recent issue of *U.S. News and World Report* could almost be a contemporary paraphrase of the words of Scripture.

Indeed, the Scripture has proclaimed for many years the power of a father, especially his failures, in a child's life. The words of Numbers 14:18 are sobering because they point out the impact of a father's failure in his child's life. "The Lord is slow to anger and abundant in lovingkindness, forgiving iniquity and transgression: but He will by no means clear the guilty, visiting the iniquity of the fathers on the children to the third and fourth generations."

While *Newsweek* magazine did not cite Scripture, the message from the article citing the influence of a father illustrates the truth of God's Word in a powerful and clear way—a child's life is greatly shaped by the example and testimony of his father. Scripture gives us a sobering reminder of the importance of the father's presence and his influence on the character of his children. Every day the truth of Numbers 14:18 is illustrated through the behavior of children mirroring what they have either experienced or seen in their biological fathers.

LOCKED UP WITH PAST FAILURES

The Dallas Morning News chronicled a moving story in a recent issue.[2] It was the incredible account of the reunion of a father and son after many years of being absent from one another. It was a moving scene when they hugged each other for the first time since the boy was a child. It was triumph and tragedy in the same moment. Why?

They met inside prison walls.

The father heard another inmate talking about a new inmate who had the same last name as his. The name was not a common one, so the father found that intriguing. He quietly hoped in his private thoughts that he would meet the new inmate.

Once he found him, he began to ask him very simple questions. "Did you live in (this town)?" The son answered the first question with a "Yes." The older inmate's heart began to beat faster.

"What street did you live on?" He answered the second question and gave a street name the older inmate was familiar with. The veteran inmate's face began to perspire profusely.

"Was your mother's name . . . ?" As the young man answered the last question with the name of the older inmate's wife, the inmate knew with certainty that this was indeed his son. This was the son he never had the opportunity to know as a person.

His adrenaline began to flow with excitement because of the realization that he was talking to his own son. This meeting also had an element of tragedy because the two men met in the most unlikely place for a father-son reunion. Inside prison walls the father now had nothing but time for the son he had never made time for when they both were free.

At least, in this instance, it appears that the father's absence had created a void in the son's life that led to a pattern of behavior that ultimately became self-destructive.

Some refer to this idea as cross-generational sin. It is a sobering principle. Dr. Kenny Ulmer expressed it in clear language when he said, "A father's traits become his children's tendencies."

GOD'S FORGIVENESS DOES NOT REMOVE THE CONSEQUENCES OF OUR SINS

Especially with fathers, the Boomerang Principle seems to apply to the daily decisions of our lives. What is the Boomerang Principle?

"What goes around, comes around."

I remember my experiences with friends who had boomerangs. No matter how far the boomerang was thrown, after it went through its spinning motion it came back somewhere near the feet of the person who had released it. There is an equally reliable life principle related to character formation in the lives of our children. The boomerang of the personal example we set before our children will ultimately come back to us in the pattern of their lives when they reach full maturity. Our actions matter.

It is no overstatement to say that we are our children's bible. They read us every day. Just as the law of gravity (what goes up must come down) remains firmly fixed, so the law of sowing and reaping (you reap what you sow) has to be reckoned with by all men. The simplicity, yet certainty, of Scripture issues a caution to all serious fathers. "Do not be deceived, God is not mocked; for whatever a man sows, this he will also reap" (Galatians 6:7).

One preacher put it in simple language, speaking of the long arm of God's judgment: "You can run, but you cannot hide."

OUR SINS DO NOT STOP WITH US

The statistics are compelling. The hardship children face who come from families where the father did not assume responsibility for leadership and support is stunning. Whether you look at the juvenile court records or the roster of an adult prison, the consistent evidence of the destructive impact of an absent father on families screams for attention. Our stewardship of the lives of those around us cannot be overestimated.

We sometimes get confused about what matters. We sometimes focus on making an impact on the world—having our names on cards and doors—rather than on using our lives to shape the character of our children and leave our "love prints" on their hearts. We will have an impact. The question is, What kind of impact will it be? The pages of Scripture give classic illustrations of how the tendencies of one generation can become the character traits of another. Looking at the tale of three generations of men from one family line dramatically demonstrates how cracks in our personal character can become gaping holes in the characters of our children.

Abraham

First we see a critical flaw in the character of Abraham.

> Now Abraham journeyed from there toward the land of the Negev, and settled between Kadesh and Shur; then he sojourned in Gerar. Abraham said of Sarah his wife, "She is my sister." So Abimilech king of Gerar sent and took Sarah. But God came to Abimelech in a dream of the night, and said to him, "Behold, you are a dead man because of the woman whom you have taken, for she is married." Now Abimilech had not come near her; and he said, "Lord, will You slay a nation, even though blameless? Did he not himself say to me, 'She is my sister'? And she herself said, 'He is my brother.' In the integrity of my heart and the innocence of my hands I have done this." Then God said to him in the dream, "Yes, I know that in the integrity of your heart you have done this, and I have kept you from sinning against Me; therefore I did not let you touch her. Now therefore, restore the man's wife, for he is a prophet, and he will pray for you and you will live. But if you do not restore her, know that you shall surely die, you and all who are yours." (Genesis 20:1–7)

Abraham let the end justify the means. He made a snap decision because it was convenient. He had a serious problem with honesty when he was put under pressure.

Abraham's experience teaches us that our personal failures impact not only us, but generations to come hang in the balance with our attitudes and actions. Character flaws may not stop with one generation. Carelessness in how we handle the circumstances in our lives that put us under pressure could harvest character flaws for generations. The children of our children depend on us to lay the foundation and set the pace for their spiritual vitality and personal well-being. There are children yet to be born whose lives will be shaped by what we do today.

If we follow the family of Abraham, we see how the trait of dishonesty in Abraham became a tendency not only in his own children, but in his children's children.

Abraham's son Isaac

This principle is clearly illustrated when we take a look at how Abraham's son Isaac responded under pressure. Abraham's tendency to fudge the truth showed up when Isaac felt his personal well-being was in jeopardy.

> Now there was a famine in the land, besides the previous famine that had occurred in the day of Abraham. So Isaac went to Gerar, to Abimilech king of the Philistines. The Lord appeared to him and said, "Do not go down to Egypt; stay in the land of which I shall tell you. Sojourn in this land and I will be with you and bless you, for to you and to your descendants I will give all these lands, and I will establish the oath which I swore to your father Abraham. I will multiply your descendants as the stars of heaven, and will give your descendants all these lands, and by your descendants all the nations of the earth shall be blessed; because Abraham obeyed Me and kept My charge, My commandments, My statutes, and My laws."
>
> So Isaac lived in Gerar. When the men of the place asked about his wife, he said, "She is my sister," for he was afraid to say, "my wife," thinking, "the men of the place might kill me on account of Rebekah, for she is beautiful." It came about, when he had been there a long time, that Abimelech . . . called Isaac and said, "Behold, certainly she is your wife! How then did you say, 'she is my sister'?" And Isaac said to him, "Because I said, 'I might die on account of her.'" Abimelech said, "What is this you have done to us? One of the people might easily have lain with your wife, and you would have brought guilt upon us." So Abimelech charged all the people, saying, "He who touches this man or his wife shall surely be put to death." (Genesis 26:1–11)

When Isaac faced a pressure situation similar to the one Abraham faced, he reacted in almost the same way his father did. Isaac wasn't yet born when Abraham lied to Abimelech about Sarah, but Isaac developed the same tendency that his father Abraham may have modeled for him as he watched him handle other challenges in life.

Isaac's son Jacob

Tragically, the tendency to fudge the truth under pressure in the lives of Abraham and Isaac surfaced as a defining characteristic in the life of Isaac's son Jacob. Jacob developed a reputation as a deceiver. Perhaps the place this tendency was most dramatically demonstrated in Abraham's family was when Jacob stole his brother Esau's blessing.

> Now it came about, when Isaac was old and his eyes were too dim to see, that he called his older son Esau and said to him, "My son." And he said to him, "Here I am." Isaac said, "Behold now, I am old and I do not know the day of my death. Now then, please take your gear, your quiver and your bow, and go out to the field and hunt game for me; and prepare a savory dish for me such as I love, and bring it to me that I may eat, so that my soul may bless you before I die."
>
> Rebekah was listening while Isaac spoke to his son Esau. So when Esau went to the field to hunt for game to bring home, Rebekah said to her son Jacob, "Behold, I heard your father speak to your brother Esau, saying, 'Bring me some game and prepare a savory dish for me, that I may eat, and bless you in the presence of the Lord before my death.' Now therefore, my son, listen to me as I command you. Go now to the flock and bring me two choice young goats from there, that I may prepare them as a savory dish for your father, such as he loves. Then you shall bring it to your father, that he may eat, so that he may bless you before his death." Jacob answered his mother Rebekah, "Behold, Esau my brother is a hairy man and I am a smooth man. Perhaps my father will feel me, then I will be as a deceiver in his sight, and I will bring upon myself a curse and not a blessing." But his mother said to him, "Your curse be on me, my son; only obey my voice, and go, get them for me." So he went and got them, and brought them to his mother; and his mother made savory food such as his father loved. Then Rebekah took the best garments of Esau her elder son, which were with her in the house, and put them on Jacob her younger son. And she put the skins of the young goats on his hands and on the smooth part of his neck. She also gave the savory food and the bread, which she had made, to her son Jacob.

> Then he came to his father and said, "My father." And he said, "Here I am. Who are you, my son?" Jacob said to his father, "I am Esau your first-born; I have done as you told me. Get up, please, sit and eat of my game, that you may bless me." (Genesis 27:1–19)

Jacob's mother put him under pressure to lie. He yielded. Jacob extended the family tradition started by his grandfather, Abraham, and continued by his father, Isaac. When the pressure came, truth was sacrificed on the altar of expediency for Abraham, his son, and his grandson.

Jacob's sons

What a tragedy! But the story does not stop there. Let's look just a little further into the lineage of Abraham. The actions of Jacob's sons in their treatment of their brother Joseph provide an interesting window into the power of a great-grandfather's actions.

> So it came about, when Joseph reached his brothers, that they stripped Joseph of his tunic, the varicolored tunic that was on him; and they took him and threw him into the pit. Now the pit was empty, without any water in it.
>
> Then they sat down to eat a meal. And as they raised their eyes and looked, behold, a caravan of Ishmaelites was coming from Gilead, with their camels bearing aromatic gum and balm and myrrh, on their way to bring them down to Egypt. Judah said to his brothers, "What profit is it for us to kill our brother and cover up his blood? Come let us sell him to the Ishmaelites and not lay our hands on him, for he is our brother, our own flesh." And his brothers listened to him. Then some Midianite traders passed by, so they pulled him up and lifted Joseph out of the pit, and sold him to the Ishmaelites for twenty shekels of silver. Thus they brought Joseph into Egypt.
>
> Now Reuben returned to the pit, and behold, Joseph was not in the pit; so he tore his garments. He returned to his brothers and said, "The boy is not there; as for me, where am I to go?" So they took Joseph's tunic, and slaughtered a male goat and dipped the tunic in the blood; and they sent the varicolored tunic and brought it to their father and said, "We found this; please examine it to see whether it is your son's tunic or not." Then he examined it and said, "It is my son's tunic. A wild beast has devoured him; Joseph has been torn to pieces!" (Genesis 37:23–33)

The boomerang principle was really at work here. Jacob had deceived his father, and now Jacob's sons deceived him. Jacob reaped what he had sown years earlier. Abraham's sin of deception was visited on the third and fourth generations. The biblical example of what happened in the experience of Abraham, Isaac, Jacob, and Jacob's sons communicates a powerful truth:

A father's example can be passed from his children to his children's children and become the defining characteristic of their lives.

This truth does not have to be viewed from a negative perspective. Instead, it can become the motivator for us to act in light of the opportunities being a fathering provides.

THE OPPORTUNITIES OF FATHERHOOD

How do we capture the powerful impact a father has on his children and convert it into a tool to shape godly character? We do so by *seizing the opportunities fathering provides.* What are they?

A powerful opportunity to model (Deuteronomy 6:1–11)

Children need to see lives worth imitating. Fathering offers a wonderful opportunity to give children an example of God's character walking, talking, and living in time and space.

One of the greatest challenges of fatherhood is illustrating and communicating the truths of God's Word so that our children respect and respond to them appropriately.

Walter Harvey will always hold a special place in my heart because I have had a chance to witness his quiet but powerful model firsthand. He happens to be the father of Annie Harvey Mercer, my wife. When Annie and I were in the early years of our relationship, one Sunday morning just before breakfast, Walter Harvey modeled for me what it means to "teach children when they rise up." As each one of his children sitting around the breakfast table recited a verse of Scripture followed by their father's prayer, I saw the Scripture communicated and illustrated. There was no fanfare, just family faith lived out one person, one day at a time.

Even today, Walter Harvey is one of my heroes. My wife is going through a literal battle for her life, as she is being treated for breast cancer. Annie has told me a number of times that one of the things that keeps her going in the middle of the night when the pain is so great she can't stand it are the verses she memorized as a child sitting at the table in the home of Walter Harvey. Those daily doses of biblical truth are medicine for the soul of my wife during some of her most challenging days. Thank God for a father-in-law who has lived out a simple faith that still proclaims a powerful daily message in the heart of my wife and our family.

Take the challenge by making sure the children in your household have a father or a surrogate they can emulate.

A powerful opportunity to mentor (Proverbs 3, 7)

"Seeing is believing." That popular phrase is especially true in the life of a young child. Children are influenced in a powerful way by the witness of a life well lived.

> *Life has some dangerous zones, times, and people; a father has the privilege and responsibility of giving insight to his children to help them recognize and avoid destructive places, times, and people.*

Every day we live provides an opportunity to give a child insight on how to deal with the danger zones and the people who will threaten his chance of fulfilling God's plan for his life.

The name Jesse W. Forbes is still respected in Camden, North Carolina, even though he died almost thirty years ago. He was not a politician, nor was he a preacher. He was simply a farmer who presented a life worth imitating in the public square and privately in his home on Trotman Road in Camden.

That's where I got to see him up close during my childhood. For me, Jesse W. Forbes, my mother's father, was the epitome of what a child would dream of in a grandfather. He was a powerful mentor on many days to me. I got a chance to see him live day in and day out supporting and caring for his family with grace and class. He navigated life with character and conviction. That's what a mentor does—he gives the children who follow him a life worth imitating. An effective father does not live a perfect life, but he does give them a life worth imitating.

A powerful opportunity to minister (Ephesians 6:4)

Show up. That's a huge part of the challenge for the average father. Unfortunately, sometimes we struggle with putting so much time into our work that our children are on the back burner. An effective father has to decide that his children are so important that he will make time on a daily basis to dedicate himself to their needs. The story, "Being Father," captures the heart cry of so many children who have aching hearts because their father is so busy.

BEING FATHER

The man came home from work late again, tired and irritated, to find his five-year-old son waiting for him at the door.

"Daddy, may I ask you a question?"

"Yeah, sure, what is it?" replied the man.

"Daddy, how much money do you make an hour?"

"That's none of your business! What makes you ask such a thing?" the man said angrily.

"I just want to know. Please tell me, how much do you make an hour?" pleaded the little boy.

"If you must know, I make $20.00 an hour."

"Oh," the little boy sighed, head bowed. Looking up, he asked,

"Daddy, may I borrow $10.00 please?"

The father was furious. "If the only reason you wanted to know how much money I make is just so you can borrow some money to buy a silly toy or some other nonsense, then you march yourself straight to your room and go to bed. Think about why you're being so selfish. I work long, hard hours every day and don't have time for such childish games."

The little boy quietly went to his room and shut the door.

The man sat down and started to get even madder about the little boy's questions. How dare he ask such questions only to get some money.

After an hour or so, the man calmed down, and started to think he may have been a little hard on his son. Perhaps, there was something his son really needed to buy with that $10.00—and he really didn't ask for money very often. The man went to the door of the boy's room and opened it.

"Are you asleep son?" he asked.

"No, Daddy. I'm awake," replied the boy.

"I've been thinking, maybe I was too hard on you earlier," said the man. "It's been a long day and I took my aggravation out on you. Here's the $10.00 you asked for."

The little boy sat straight up beaming. "Oh, thank you Daddy!" he exclaimed. Then reaching under his pillow, he pulled out some crumpled up bills.

The man, seeing that the boy already had money, started to get angry again. The little boy slowly counted out his money, then looked up at his dad.

"Why did you want more money if you already had some?" the father demanded.

"Because I didn't have enough, but now I do," the little boy replied.

"Daddy, I have $20.00 now. Can I buy an hour of your time?"

An effective father gives children ample portions of his time at no cost to them.

A powerful opportunity to be a messenger for God (1 Samuel 2:12–4:22)

It is hard to tell someone you love that he is wrong. It can come across as harsh and judgmental, and no one wants to sound like that. But a true understanding of the father's role as messenger can make the fear of being judgmental fade away. God's standards are given to us so that we can avoid some of the land mines and quicksand that can trap our family every day.

Failure to respond to God's standards can bring severe consequences. A godly father has the responsibility to set and maintain boundaries for the behavior of the children under his responsibility.

The biblical example of how God responded to the Old Testament priest Eli offers a sobering reminder of how important it is for a father to fulfill his responsibility to warn his children of the consequences of their actions when they are outside God's will.

The Scriptures describe Eli's sons as "worthless men; they did not know the Lord and the custom of the priests with the people" (1 Samuel 2:12–13). They took more of the sacrifice than would have been their portion as priests, they took the meat before the fat had been burned as a sacrifice to God, and, in general, they "despised the offering of the Lord" (vv. 13–17). They also "lay with the women who served at the doorway of the tent of meeting" (v. 22).

Although it is not pleasant, discipline is an important part of a father's responsibility to his children, and Eli failed in this duty. He knew what his sons were doing and yet he did nothing. Destruction came upon his family as a result. Both of his sons were killed in battle in a single day, and the ark of God was taken by the Philistines (1 Samuel 4:10–12). When Eli heard the news that the ark had been taken, he "fell off the seat backward beside the gate, and his neck was broken and he died" (v. 18).

I will never forget the experience of a prominent Christian leader in a time in the life of his family where one of his children had made a choice that dishonored God and brought embarrassment to her family. Instead of hiding the sin of his child, this leader had his daughter make a public confession of her sin before the congregation of his church. This took incredible courage and conviction. It was clear that the family did not stop loving and caring for this child, but everyone watching knew the father had communicated God's standards and the consequences of personal sin to her.

Hearing the words of confession from that daughter made it clear that she had heard the truth and seen it modeled in the home of her parents. She still had chosen to disobey, and now she was experiencing and had come to understand the consequences on a totally different level. Hearing this child share her testimony was a sobering reminder to me that we have to deliver the message even when we know our children are not listening. A father's challenge is to give his children boundaries and limits with a spirit of love and gentleness and, when they don't listen, be a messenger of God ready to make sure they learn from the consequences of their mistakes. Perhaps that is one of the most powerful demonstrations of love a father can display.

KEEP SAYING THOSE POWERFUL WORDS

It is pretty amazing how powerful three simple words are. I know how important they are to me. Annie had taken our young kids out so I could have the house to myself for some last minute polishing of a sermon I had to deliver the next morning. I was deep in reflection and study when the phone rang.

It was a very familiar voice on a long-distance call. It was my father. My hometown newspaper in North Carolina had run a press release about a recent promotion I had just received to an executive position in a prominent ministry in the Dallas area. The conversation was short, but I still feel the impact in my spirit years later.

"How are you doing?" "Fine," I responded. Then his words taught me something about myself. "I read about your promotion . . . I am very proud of you and—I love you."

The words "I love you" kept echoing in the hollow parts of my heart. Certainly he had said those words before, but somehow in that moment they seemed so fresh and new to me.

Before I put the phone down, my hand and wrist were wet and warm, not with sweat, but with tears. Somehow, those words had unlocked a part of my heart that held pent-up feelings that now came rushing out. In that brief moment, as I mumbled out a "Thank you," my heart felt a deep sense of relief. I hung up the phone and deep sobs came flowing out of me; I knew how powerful those words really are.

I made the commitment that day—to God with my words and to my children in my heart—that saying "I love you" would be my gift to them every day when we have contact with each other.

FAITH STEPS

1. Realize that your actions are always before the watchful eye of God (Psalm 139).

2. Remember that your words and deeds can shape the character of your children (Proverbs 4:1–5:14).

3. Reflect on the fact that you are living a pattern for generations to come (Psalm 78).

4. Give your children the gift of truth that will last forever (Proverbs 2:1–3:12).

5. Commit yourself to the daily nurturing of your children in truth, experiences, and exposure that will help them develop godly character (Proverbs 7:1–4).

A PARENT'S PRAYER

Dear Lord, Thank You for the powerful example a father's life has on the development of his children. Give my child the example of a life worth imitating in his father. Give my child a model, mentor, minister, and messenger as a father. Give my child the gift of those mystical words—"I love you"—from his father every day. Thank You I don't have to be perfect, but simply faithful. Help my child experience the power of a faithful father. Amen.

PARENTING INSIGHTS

SPECIAL CARE INSTRUCTIONS

Research Highlight: The Challenges of Boyhood

Boyhood offers unique challenges in America particularly. Your knowledge of these special circumstances can greatly enhance your ability to helps the boys in your life reach their full potential under Christ.[3]

RESEARCH HIGHLIGHTS

- Birth defects strike boys a lot more than they do girls, and some two hundred genetic diseases affect only boys.
- Boys are talked to less than girls and are more likely to be held facing away from the parent than are girls.
- The incidence of Attention Deficit/Hyperactivity Disorder (ADHD) is diagnosed almost exclusively with males. Five out of six adolescents diagnosed with ADHD are male.
- Boys are admitted to mental hospitals and juvenile institutions seven times more than girls of similar age and social circumstances.
- More than 85 percent of adolescent discipline problems in schools are with boys.
- Violent crimes involve males as victims much more than females because they fifteen times more likely to be victims than their female counterparts.
- Females are four times less likely to commit suicide than adolescent males.

RESEARCH APPLICATIONS

These observations from research should challenge each parent to intensify his efforts to make sure the boys he has influence over are given the opportunity to succeed.

1. Recognize the unique challenges boys face in contemporary society.
2. Make sure each boy has at least one positive adult male role model in his life that he can call in times of personal crises.
3. Protect your child from inappropriate diagnosis, assessment, and/or characterization of his behavior.
4. Give each boy the same level of nurturing that girls receive during the early years of their lives.
5. Create a positive peer culture around each boy to foster godly attitudes and actions in a supportive environment.
6. Encourage each boy every day with affirmations based on his personal character and worth to God.
7. Ensure that each boy has someone praying with and for him every day.

"My son, do not forget my teaching, But let your heart keep my commandments; For length of days and years of life And peace they will add to you" (Proverbs 3:1–2).

If boys are to be the kind of husbands and fathers we want them to be, we need to convert the challenges into character-building tools for each boy soon to become a man.

10

WRAP IN RIGHTEOUSNESS

The Christian Home: God's Platform for Developing Character

"Talking walls?" Yes. You read it right. Talking walls. One of the most powerful tools God has given us to cultivate godly character in the lives of our children could be talking walls.

Let me illustrate what I mean. One evening we were having a family Bible study, and during the course of the discussion my oldest daughter made an observation that caught both Annie and me by surprise. We were amazed that she could remember and convey such an important spiritual truth in the simple language she used.

We asked her how she had come to her conclusion. She said, "I have been reading that plaque on the wall every day." Over the years, Annie has always made it a practice to have verses of Scripture and other spiritual messages on the walls and tables of our home. She has tried to create what we call "a spiritual life laboratory." We want our children to bump into truth about God wherever they go in the home.

We believe there are ways we can apply the principles Moses communicated in Deuteronomy 6:6–9 to our home environment today.

> "These words, which I am commanding you today, shall be on your heart. You shall teach them diligently to your sons and shall talk of them when you sit in your house and when you walk by the way and when you lie down and when you rise up. You shall bind them as a sign on your hand and they shall be as frontals on your forehead. You shall write them on the doorposts of your house and on your gates."

Your home can be an incubator of physical, emotional, social, intellectual, and spiritual development for your children. This passage in Deuteronomy shows one way to do that. Moses was challenging the Jewish parents to create the kind of environment that consistently pointed the attention of their children toward God so that they could reach their full personal potential.

While many things are different today from what they were when these verses were originally written, the opportunity to use the home environment as a place of spiritual instruction remains available to us. School is a neat place, but it does not take the place of the home. Church is important to the development of children, but growth occurs most consistently when it is cultivated by godly parents in a home committed to God. The first question we need to answer is, How do we go about doing that?

PRESENT SIGHTS, SOUNDS, AND SYMBOLS THAT HONOR GOD

For my family, that has meant a commitment to making sure no music plays in the household that promotes values inconsistent with what we having been teaching our children. I do not operate under the illusion that my children will never be exposed to music that attacks the teaching of Scripture. I do not operate under the idealistic perspective that my children will never see pornographic images in literature or in movies. I simply have committed to make sure that does not happen with our approval as parents in our home.

That commitment has one overarching purpose: to establish the home as a place where purity is promoted and the environment is protected from the onslaught of ideas and images that dishonor God. Of course, this is becoming increasingly more difficult as the standards of television keep decreasing and more and more images used to sell products promote sex outside of marriage and other values that do not reflect the standards of Scripture. That commitment also means filling the home atmosphere with positive, wholesome, entertaining music. That means working hard at finding good alternatives for the best the world has to offer.

Being a committed Christian doesn't mean your home has to be boring and dull. There are a lot of good musical choices and artistic options that can be both enjoyable and pure. Work at it. But how do you keep those pictures, posters, and artwork from simply being religious artifacts on your walls? How do you keep that music from being just a combination of religious sounds? I believe it starts with the attitude we have toward our homes.

DEDICATE YOURSELF TO PROVIDING SPIRITUAL LEADERSHIP FOR YOUR FAMILY

You first have to give the home and those who live there back to God. Although you are making the house payments, it is important that you understand that the house, apartment, or other dwelling where you live—along with all who live there—are available to God for His use. Joshua 24:15 captures the spirit of dedication we should have toward our households, as it uses the term *house* to refer to the entire family.

> "If it is disagreeable in your sight to serve the Lord, choose for yourselves today whom you will serve: whether the gods which your fathers served which were beyond the River, or the gods of the Amorites in whose land you are living; but as for me and my house, we will serve the Lord."

Make it clear to your children that you want everything about your family to be dedicated to God's service—and that includes making your house a place that honors God. Your children and all who visit your home need to know there are limits on the things that will happen there. But that raises the question, How do we do that practically? It starts with a simple but demanding commitment.

COMMIT TO MAKING YOUR HOUSE A PLACE OF RIGHTEOUSNESS

Decide that your home will be a place of righteousness. If you do that, you can count on God's presence and His blessing to be there. The writer of the book of Proverbs understood that: "The curse of the Lord is on the house of the wicked, but He blesses the dwelling of the righteous" (Proverbs 3:33).

What does that mean? Will it be perfect in your house? No, not as long as people live there. But your home can be a place where you let your children and all who enter know by the environment you create that your heart's desire is that God would be pleased to sit down at your table any time He chooses to—and feels at home. You do that by asking yourself a simple question: *Would Jesus be comfortable in my home with this movie on, or this music playing, or while we are engaged in this activity?*

Righteousness in the life of a child does not happen by osmosis or by accident. It is the result of an intentional process. It happens over the day-in, day-out routine. Your home can be a place where you can focus on developing righteousness in your child's life one day at a time.

If you create that kind of environment, you will make your home an attractive place to be. That will give you the platform for some wonderful times of ministry to your child and others.

SHARE YOUR HOME WITH OTHERS TO TEACH YOUR CHILD COMPASSION AND COMPANIONSHIP

Opening up your home to family friends and your child's peers will not only help her learn how to build relationships, but also to show her how to express God's love for others who face challenging situations. We have had the privilege of hosting a number of missionaries and servants of the Lord over the years. Our children have had the privilege of seeing some of God's choice servants and learning from them as they talked with them around the breakfast table or during dinner.

The Scripture gives numerous illustrations of how the ministry of hospitality was important. Using your home to advance the work of God can result in great blessing. Model a ministry of compassion before your children by using your home as a place of ministry.

USE YOUR HOME TO TEACH RESPONSIBILITY

As the saying goes, "Responsibility is not taught; it is caught." Your home is an excellent place to develop a good work ethic and demonstrate the importance of making good choices and practicing biblically based decision making. If you teach your child to learn to respect other persons and personal property, that will prepare her to live successfully outside the home with other people.

The opening pages of Scripture illustrate the value God places on responsibility and work. "Then the Lord God took the man and put him into the garden of Eden to cultivate it and keep it" (Genesis 2:15). There are many points of application you can take from God's emphasis on work. One is that home can be a place where good habits are taught to your children through everyday acts of responsibility.

Annie has placed a little plaque in a prominent place in our home for everyone to see. She picked it up at a garage sale. We try to incorporate most of the home rules given in this plaque into our family routine. You may find the list helpful as you build a platform to teach your children responsibility.

HOME RULES

If you sleep on it make it up.
If you wear it hang it up.
If you drop it pick it up.
If you eat off it put it in the sink.
If you step on it wipe it off.
If you open it close it.
If you empty it fill it up.
If it rings answer it.
If it howls feed it.
If it cries love it.

Develop your own home rules for your children and then work at helping them learn responsibility by applying those rules. You will be tempted to not try to do this because it's so hard to get children to take care of the small details of their lives. But if your children don't learn to take care of details at home, it will be a real challenge for them to develop those positive habits as adults.

BUILD MEMORIES THAT WILL LAST YOUR CHILDREN FOR A LIFETIME

One of the most powerful things you can do for your child is build memories that will last a lifetime. Be aware of what you want your child to think and feel when she leaves your home, and work on it every day. Your child won't remember the "big" gifts you give her as much as she will the everyday things you do to invest in her personal maturity and development.

For us that has meant times of prayer and Bible study, but it has also meant family dinners and water gun fights with Aunt Princess and Uncle David. It has meant time for quiet reflection as a family, but it has also meant rich times of fellowships with close friends who have reached a kind of declared relative status: "Uncle Grover and Aunt Sharon, and Uncle Leonard, and Aunt Margaret." Those names sure do reflect powerful and positive memories.

The main thing is that you make memories your children can reflect on when they think about growing up in your home. Yes, one of the memories we are committed to leaving on the hearts of our children is beginning and ending each day with prayer, hopefully with plenty of joy and growth in between. But we also committed to making sure all the activity of homes everywhere can contribute to blessed memories. I wrote a simple prayer that pictures key elements of a Christian home. It does not have to be a perfect place. But home can be a place of blessed memories. That is what this prayer will hopefully lead all of our hearts toward as parents. It is called "A Prayer for Blessed Memories," and it is my sincere prayer for you.

A PRAYER FOR BLESSED MEMORIES

I pray that blessed memories will come when my child reflects on his time at home.

Yes. I want the times of prayer to be a blessing,
But the times of play at home should be blessing too.

Blessed memories—that is what I want my child's thoughts about home to be.

Yes. I want the times of Bible study to be a blessing,
But times of lively chatter in the home should be a blessing too.

Blessed memories—that is what I want my child's thoughts about home to be.

Yes. I want the times of peace and privacy to be a blessing,
But using the home as a place of hospitality and fellowship with friends should be a blessing too.

Blessed memories—that is what I want my child's thoughts about home to be.

Yes. I want the holidays and special occasions to be a blessing,
But the love expressed in the home during normal, routine, and uneventful days should be a blessing too.

Blessed memories—that is what I want my child's thoughts about home to be.

Yes. I want times of victory and success to be a blessing,
But since love in the home is not conditional, times of disappointment and failure can be a blessing too.

Yes. I want the times of pleasure and prosperity to be a blessing.
But a godly home during times of hardship and pain can be used by God to bring a blessing too.

Blessed memories—that is what I want my child's thoughts about home to be.

At all times, and under all circumstances, I pray that my child's thoughts about home will bring blessed memories.

Amen.

FAITH STEPS

1. Make a commitment that the things that are said and done in your home are going to honor God.

2. Place sights, sounds, and symbols in your home that honor God.

3. Practice hospitality in your home so that your child sees your commitment to using your home as a place of blessing and ministry to others.

4. Keep the airwaves (television, music) pure so that if your child learns unwholesome things it would not have happened in your home.

5. Establish a "family altar" in your home by regularly leading your family in worship and Bible study.

A PARENT'S PRAYER

Father, Thank You that You have given me a home to provide a place of safety and protection. Give me the strength to use this house to teach my child to love and worship You. Help me keep the environment safe from harm and danger for my child and free of messages that will compromise her commitment to You. Bring people to this house who will model godly character before my child. Keep people away from this house who will dishonor Your name and distract my child from worshiping You. Bless this house, O Lord, with Your righteousness. Amen.

PARENTING INSIGHTS

SPECIAL CARE INSTRUCTIONS

Research Highlight: The Impact of Divorce

Divorce has always been viewed as a challenge for everyone in the family to go through. It is very important that every parent, at least, review the devastation that divorce can have on the life of some children.[1]

RESEARCH HIGHLIGHTS

- A million new kids each year join the category of "children of divorce."
- Interestingly, the chance of divorce happening is highest during the third year of the marriage.
- Although some researchers believe divorce has little impact on most children, conventional wisdom holds that it has a significant long-term negative impact on the success of children.
- A significant amount of research suggests that children of divorce have a higher incidence of depression, learning difficulties, and other psychological problems.
- Family conflict, whether it leads to divorce or not, creates the potential for insecurity in the mind and heart of a child and can be a tremendous distraction to her growth and maturity.
- Children who grow up in two-parent homes are more likely to perform better in school and less likely to join a gang and get addicted to drugs.

These research results will hopefully motivate parents who live in a two-parent family to place a high priority on maintaining a strong marriage to honor God and give a supportive environment to their children.

RESEARCH APPLICATIONS

1. Make sure that one of the greatest gifts you give your child is the model of a strong marriage relationship.
2. Use your marriage relationship as a platform to teach your child how to resolve conflict in the midst of a family environment in a healthy manner.
3. Show your love for your mate in a demonstrable manner so your child will learn what it means to love a spouse passionately.
4. Pray together as a couple to teach your child how to place God at the center of the home life.
5. If you are going through a struggle as a married couple, place the needs of your child on a high enough level that you can find common points of agreement around what is in her best interest.
6. If you are separated and/or divorced, make sure you use phone calls, letters, visits, and special times in your child's life to communicate your concern and love for her.
7. Pray consistently that God will give you wisdom to make sure your marriage relationship is not a distraction to the spiritual growth of your child.

"Be kind to one another, tender-hearted, forgiving each other, just as God in Christ also has forgiven you" (Ephesians 4:32).

Ask God to make your marriage relationship a testimony to His power and grace.

11

USE MEMORY POWER

Teaching Your Children Through Life Experiences

The ninth floor of 820 North LaSalle, Chicago, Illinois, is a long way from 1216 Moseley Street, Elizabeth City, North Carolina. Not only is there is a lot of distance between those two locations, there is a wide gap between the experiences. God used both of those places to teach me about life and parenting.

1216 Moseley Street is part of Debry Courts in Elizabeth City, North Carolina. When I was growing up there, it was known as "the projects." That is what they called public housing back then. That is where I spent part of my childhood and where God taught me many unforgettable life lessons.

The ninth floor of 820 North LaSalle is where I have my office as vice president of church ministries and assistant to the president of Moody Bible Institute. It is where I have the privilege of serving the Lord with a ministry that touches millions of people in the name of Jesus. It is a place of great privilege and honor. Now, why is that important?

DON'T FORGET THE OLD NEIGHBORHOODS

There is a long distance between 1216 Moseley Street and 820 North LaSalle.

A lot of life has occurred between Moseley Street and 820 North LaSalle. God's footprints are evident all along the way. That is why where I have my office is very important. It is important because God's grace has taken me from the projects to a position in one of His choice places of ministry.

As a father, I am very much aware that God wants me to let my children know about my life and my experiences. Why? Not to exalt myself but to help them see that our future does not have to be defined by our past. It is important for my children and their children to know that whatever circumstances they find themselves in do not exceed God's capacity to work and accomplish His purpose. The distance between 1216 Moseley and 820 North LaSalle is not just geographic. It shows God can take our limitations and lift us into places our human imaginations and capabilities cannot.

God's Word gives us a powerful illustration of how important and significant our spiritual life experiences are. The specific instructions God gave Joshua for His people after they successfully crossed over the Jordan River have tremendous implications for your practice as a parent.

> Now when all the nation had finished crossing the Jordan, the Lord spoke to Joshua, saying, "Take for yourselves twelve men from the people, one man from each tribe, and command them, saying, 'Take for yourselves twelve stones from here out of the middle of the Jordan, from the place where the priests' feet are standing firm, and carry them over with you and lay them down in the lodging place where you will lodge tonight.'" So Joshua called the twelve men whom he had appointed from the sons of Israel, one man from each tribe; and Joshua said to them, "Cross again to the ark of the Lord your God into the middle of the Jordan, and each of you take up a stone on his shoulder, according to the number of the tribes of the sons of Israel. Let this be a sign among you, so that when your children ask later, saying, 'What do these stones mean to you?' then you shall say to them, 'Because the waters of the Jordan were cut off before the ark of the covenant of the Lord; when it crossed the Jordan, the waters of the Jordan were cut off.' So these stones shall become a memorial to the sons of Israel forever." (Joshua 4:1–7)

God did not want Joshua and the people to forget where they came from, nor did He want them to minimize where He had taken them. In short, He did not want them to take the place they were standing for granted. We need to make sure we don't cheat our children out of learning about the activity of God in our lives.

BUILD PLATFORMS TO TEACH CHILDREN ABOUT GOD

A record of God's faithfulness can be a great inspiration to believers going through a personal struggle. God challenged the nation of Israel to erect stones of remembrance to commemorate His activity in their lives. Those stones were intended to be practical object lessons for them from the "School of Life" to help them build their personal faith. Similar "stones" are important ways to help your children connect to God.

God wants you to learn from the instructions He gave Joshua. A major purpose of the stone-laying process in the book of Joshua was to create a platform for teaching children about God. It is interesting that God told Joshua to be ready to respond to the questions of children. I believe there is a great lesson there for parents.

We are to place things in our children's paths that spark their interest in spiritual realities. Keep your eyes open to life lessons from your experiences that you can use to create a deeper faith in God. You can do that through books, tapes, and other resources. Plant seeds that result in spiritual interest in their lives.

CREATE SOME SPECIAL MOMENTS

The sophomore year of my oldest daughter in high school was an exciting time for her. She turned sixteen, was invited to join the National Honor Society, and was listed with *Who's Who Among American High School Students.* Those were exciting moments.

But there was a moment that I hope eclipses all those nice honors. During the week of her sixteenth birthday we went out on a dinner date, as we occasionally have the opportunity to do. I had the special privilege of giving her a necklace with a special locket. As I gave her that necklace, I had the opportunity to tell her how absolutely beautiful and special she is in the eyes of God. I asked her to wear that necklace near her heart and remember that both God and I have a deep love for her.

I also challenged her to keep her heart and life pure until God gave her a husband. The locket is a symbol of love and purity. Until she is married, I am praying that God will use that locket as a symbol of love and purity on a daily basis in her life.

It may be selfish, but I am hoping that moment will be forever etched in her mind. My prayer is that it will be a memory that God will allow her to treasure for the rest of her life.

Seek opportunities to create special moments in the life of your child. Capture birthdays, holidays, and other occasions to make memories that will last.

DRAW LESSONS FROM THE GOOD AND THE BAD

This principle of using life experience as a platform for teaching our children extends beyond the experience at the crossing of the Jordan River. It includes teaching children the laws of God and the failures of those in the past so that they can avoid the mistakes of others. God illustrated this principle from a different perspective in the Psalms.

> For He established a testimony in Jacob
> And appointed a law in Israel,
> Which He commanded our fathers
> That they should teach them to their children,
> That the generations to come might know, even the children yet to be born,
> That they may arise and tell them to their children,
> That they should put their confidence in God
> And not forget the works of God,
> But keep His commandments,
> And not be like their fathers,
> A stubborn and rebellious generation,
> A generation that did not prepare its heart
> And whose spirit was not faithful to God.
>
> —Psalm 78:5–8

A testimony of God's faithfulness in the past can be a tremendous inspiration for the future. As you look at God's faithfulness in the lives of His people, it should be encouraging to you personally. It is important to know the stories that describe God's past faithfulness to help with present and future challenges.

REMEMBER THAT YOUR PERSONAL STORY IS AN IMPORTANT TOOL

Your past and present experiences with God can be powerful tools to help your child understand the presence and power of God. One of the most important stories you can relate to your child is how you came to know Jesus Christ as personal Savior. It is important that your child understands your personal salvation story.

That will take the teaching of the Bible about God's ability to save us by grace through faith off the pages of Scripture and the sanctuary of a church and into the heart of your child.

You may even (selectively) tell your child about your times of personal struggle so that he will know that God's grace is sufficient for him even when he doesn't get things right. Let him know that the truth of the first part of James 3:2, "For we all stumble in many ways," applies to you as well as to everyone else he meets.

We sometime give our children the false impression that our lives are free from any failure. If we are not careful, they will believe that in order to be accepted by God, and us, their lives have to be "perfect" too.

This kind of thinking will short-circuit your child's ability to know the wonderful gift of God's grace for us when we stumble and fall short of His perfect standard. Instead of feeling free to go to the Lord and confess, he will be prone to languish in self-condemnation and not experience the power of a personal relationship with God. Your child needs to understand that failure does not have to be fatal.

PRESERVE THE STORY OF YOUR FAMILY'S JOURNEY

Our family, like all other families, has had its share of victories and defeats. We have tried to preserve our family's personal journey for our children and their children through pictures and other mementos. We have also tried to recount to our children some personal stories about experiences in our family life where God intervened in a special way.

Give your child a glimpse of the supernatural through your life. Have there been times in your life that only can be explained by the supernatural intervention of God? If so, sharing those events with your child can make a big difference in his personal view of God. Annie and I have shared some of our experiences of God's intervention with our children so their faith could be encouraged.

One of the experiences we have shared with our children that they still marvel at was an experience we had more than twenty years ago when we were a poor, struggling seminary couple. Annie and I were trying to make ends meet on a shoestring budget. We were facing a very difficult financial crisis. We had a need for $1,700 more than we had coming in that month. We had no idea where the money was going to come from.

One day during that time of great financial stress, I came home from class and went through my normal routine, which included going to work. After I got to work that day, I received a phone call from Annie letting me know that a fellow classmate had felt led by God to come by our little apartment and drop off a check for $1,700. He had an unusual blessing from God that he wanted to share with us. He gave the gift under the condition that we never publicly tell who gave the gift. We agreed to that condition and have never mentioned this man's name in public. Although we had not shared with anyone publicly that we needed additional cash in that amount, his check was exactly what we needed.

We both praised God for His goodness. We also learned something as individual believers and a family unit that we will never forget. We became convinced that God answers prayer in a tangible, concrete manner when we are bold enough to ask Him. Our children have been told that story so that they can praise God with us and also so that they know that God can answer their prayers in the same way.

SHOW YOUR CHILDREN HOW TO CONVERT STONES INTO STEPS

One of the greatest lessons you can teach your child through your past experiences is that God can convert stones—struggles in our lives—into steps, or opportunities. I have shared with my children what I have learned about the Chinese word for crisis. It is made up of two symbols. One of those symbols represents danger. The other stands for opportunity. We have tried to teach our children to look at every crisis in their lives as not only a point of danger but a place of opportunity to see God intervene in a very special way on their behalf.

When Annie was first diagnosed with breast cancer we were, of course, traumatized at the thought of what that meant for Annie and for us as a family. But we sat down together as a family and committed to a daily prayer together for her healing. It has been a very difficult time, especially for Annie, and God is using the experience of Annie's illness to teach us all to trust Him as she has gone through surgery, chemotherapy, and radiation.

We have been fortunate to have many people express support in unbelievable ways. But we have learned as a family unit that ultimately we need to learn to lean on each other through difficult and challenging times like this. I believe this crisis has caused each family member to develop a greater appreciation for the others as a part of his personal support system.

As difficult as it is, we are trying to relate Annie's journey to wholeness as an illustration of how God works in the lives of individuals and families. Through this experience, we have had to place in perspective a lot of errant theology concerning healing and other issues a believer in Christ faces. Convert challenges in your child's life and in the experience of the family into opportunities for spiritual instruction and growth for each member of the family.

"A PICTURE IS WORTH A THOUSAND WORDS"

Dr. Anthony Evans related an interesting personal experience one Sunday morning during a sermon that illustrated how a simple picture can be very significant in the life of a child. He told the congregation about an experience with his eldest son, Anthony. He went home from work one afternoon and Anthony met him at the door and hugged him.

His son told him that he had been looking at a family photo album. He saw a picture of Dr. Evans holding him when he was an infant. His son's words were poignant. "You have been there all the time."

That picture album captured a record of a father's faithfulness. It created an opportunity for a son to express his love and appreciation. This is a great illustration of how simple things can inspire and motivate us to get serious about our personal relationships.

You can create the same kind of opportunities to bond with your children by learning to capture the special moments in your child's life experience through pictures and symbols. I love the way my wife has reflected that reality by hanging pictures throughout our house that capture special memories and moments in our experience as a family.

Fill the walls and halls of your house with pictures and other images that capture memories of God's work in your life as individuals and as a family. Those pictures and images will call out to your children on a daily basis while they are in your home that God has been at work in your life as a family. Hopefully, the greatest message will be that God wants to be at work in their lives as they leave your home and raise their own families.

ALWAYS REMEMBER, DON'T FORGET, AND LOOK AHEAD

My oldest son wrote this poem for his peers as he was finishing his senior year in high school. This is one of the clearest descriptions of the power of memory I have ever seen. It shows how memory can help preserve the past and give direction for the future.

ALWAYS REMEMBER, DON'T FORGET, AND LOOK AHEAD

As our last years begin to wind down,
Take a chance to stop and look around.
Always remember all the good times you've had,
Always remember these along with the bad.

Always remember the many friendships begun,
And the lost friends that have been won.
Always remember those who have passed along,
In our hearts they will always belong.

USE MEMORY POWER

Always remember the memories shared
By both us and those who cared.
Always remember those bygone years,
The thought of which can't help but bring tears,

Don't forget those who have gone before,
Whose achievements have helped open the door.
Don't forget to say a heartfelt thank you,
To those who have always been and will always be there for you.

Don't forget what you stand for,
Your faith will become important to you more and more.
Don't forget the one up above,
Who is looking down upon you in love.

Don't forget all those back home,
They're still important even though you're all grown.
Don't forget to show your parents that you care.
It would surprise you how little they are aware.

Look ahead to being alone,
For now you're on your own.
Look ahead to brand-new freedom,
It's what these past twelve years have won.

Look ahead to new places and things,
But beware of the dangers they bring,
Look ahead to new relationships,
But be sure they don't cause you to trip.

Look ahead to Christ taking more steps with you,
He'll be there for you through and through.
Look ahead to lots of prayer,
That will help you always beware.

You think you've experienced everything;
Well, surprise, life has plenty more to bring.
Just keep this close to your heart,
And you'll be off to a great start.
Always Remember, Don't Forget, and Look Ahead.

FAITH STEPS

1. Write out your own personal testimony of how you came to know Christ, and share it with your child.
2. Keep a record of God's significant interventions in your life and tell your child the stories as he grows.
3. Regularly share with your child the special things you are trusting God to do.
4. Create your own personal and family symbols to commemorate special events and seasons in your life.
5. Collect special pictures and other memorabilia to mark seasons in your life that have special personal and spiritual significance.

A PARENT'S PRAYER

Father, Thank You for giving me my own personal testimony to share with my child. Help me to never take for granted Your special intervention in my life. Help me share with my child the wonderful things I am asking You to do in my life. Grant me the insight I need to capture special moments that mark Your special presence in my life. Amen.

PARENTING INSIGHTS

SPECIAL CARE INSTRUCTIONS

Research Highlight: The Computer and Your Child

The computer is serving as a wonderful tool for learning, research, business, and personal growth and development. But like any other significant resource; it has great potential to be misused by people with evil intent. Some interesting observations can be made as we look at what the research is telling us about computer use for your children.[1]

RESEARCH HIGHLIGHTS

- Approximately 7 million teenagers log on to the Internet every day.
- There are literally thousands of helpful Web sites available to assist children and teens in finding helpful information for school and personal growth.
- In a recent TIME/CNN, poll more than 69 percent of the children surveyed indicated their parents either had rules they did not follow or did not have rules for Internet use.
- More than 44 percent of teenagers surveyed in a TIME/CNN poll indicated they had visited Web sites that are X-rated or have sexual content.
- More than 58 percent teens surveyed on Internet use indicated they have encountered people on line who wanted personal information, such as their address and/or phone number.
- There are a number of possible dangers facing children on the Internet, including either sites or people who are focused on materialism, pedophilia, pornography, racism, or violence.

RESEARCH APPLICATIONS

1. Become informed about the benefits and dangers the computer and Internet bring.
2. Get on the offensive and structure your child's use of the computer and Internet by developing a "Family Computer Use Covenant" that restricts your child from harmful Web sites.
3. Put the computer in a prominent and visible place so you can see what your child is doing.
4. Use filterware or software applications that can block things that could harm your child.
5. Monitor your child's use of the computer and the sites he visits when on the Internet.
6. Train your child how to respond to potentially deceptive people or information on the Internet.
7. Equip your child with the information and encouragement he needs to use the Internet and computer correctly, or give him positive alternatives.

"We are destroying speculations and every lofty thing raised up against the knowledge of God, and we are taking every thought captive to the obedience of Christ" (2 Corinthians 10:5).

There are a number of ways you can use this research to maximize the benefits of this wonderful technology for the benefit of your child. Seize them for God's glory.

12

KEEP IN SAFE PLACES

Monitoring Social Influences on Your Child's Life

She is affectionately called "Lil Sis" by her family and many young women, including my wife, who have been touched by her life. Her given name is Fannie Griffin-Mann. I really don't know where the name "Lil Sis" came from because she is not unusually small in stature. I think of Fannie Griffin-Mann as a woman of God who has been a surrogate mother to a lot of children. Many of them spent so much time at her home that it was like a home away from home for them. A lot of children spent many hours around her kitchen table learning about God and simple life lessons.

In fact, she carried the official title "Mother of the Church" at her church and many other churches when her health was strong enough to enable her to travel and encourage young women to be good mothers. When she was more active, everywhere she went her commitment to God, love of people, and life worth imitating left a trail of spiritual impact.

I remember hearing her reflect with a note of sadness that God didn't allow her to give birth to her own children. God had another plan for her life. God chose to give her more "children of faith" than she could possibly have given birth to herself. The extent of her life impact will only be measured in eternity.

Now that she is in her late seventies, many adult women bring their young girls by and say thanks to "Lil Sis" for being a positive influence in their life away from home. Thank God that she extended her spiritual influence so unselfishly in the lives of so many people.

I am thankful that one of those people is the woman I have been married to for more than twenty years. When we go back home, one of the places we stop is the home of "Lil Sis."

All children need people like "Lil Sis" in their lives. All children need people in their lives when they are away from home who will love them and encourage them to do the right thing as they face life's challenges. I am convinced that God has placed people like that around for every child.

During the course of your child's life, she will spend a large amount of time away from you. Much of that time, you will have to simply entrust your child to the protection and care of God, for no matter how much you try, your control will be very limited. During those times of separation, your prayer life is the greatest tool you have to invest in the maturity and development of your child.

But when you can shape the influences of others in your child's life, it is important to take that very seriously. It is imperative that you take very seriously your stewardship of the exposure your child has to godly influences.

THE LIFE OF A GODLY TEACHER CAN BE A POWERFUL INFLUENCE

When I was a young boy, Mr. Sylvester would drive up to my home very faithfully every Sunday morning with his brown two-toned station wagon and crowd me, along with a few other boys, into his car. Then we traveled the short ride off to Sunday school at Cornerstone Baptist Church. What did I learn from Sunday school class? I am embarrassed to say that not many topics come to my mind from the Sunday school materials.

Most of my lessons were learned just by seeing Mr. Sylvester show up every week. Though I am sure he was a very good teacher in the classroom,

I learned more on the way to church in the car. He made a lasting impact on my spiritual formation at an important stage in my life as a child. He simply showed up on a regular basis to invest in my life.

Cherish opportunities to let your children learn from teachers in the church educational program. Get them involved in activities that are designed to encourage their spiritual growth. Sure, they will learn from the structured teaching time, but one of ways God will impact them most will be by letting them rub shoulders with other committed Christian adults who model the Christian life for them. Pray that during their childhood experience under your stewardship God will provide them with a teacher who has a "life worth imitating." In fact, seek out people who can be an extension of your ministry to your children.

POSITIVE TEACHERS AND MENTORS CAN MAKE A PROFOUND DIFFERENCE

Many people are very critical of teachers, especially those who serve in public schools. I am sure there are some teachers who deserve the criticism, just like there are some doctors, lawyers, and ministers who disgrace their profession. But it is very unfair to place all public school teachers in one group as incompetent and uncaring. Actually, they deserve our respect much more than our criticism.

Some of the finest servants of God I know are laboring for God in the public schools of our community. I reflect back with fondness on some of my elementary, junior high, and high school teachers who looked past my problems and saw some sort of potential in me. They had a very significant impact on my life.

I am so thankful to the Lord that He has allowed my children to be exposed to positive powerful people of faith, like Joann Das, an elementary school teacher, and Juanita Browder, a former principal and now administrator. These women are unsung heroes in the halls of schools and have just as significant a ministry where they are as any teacher in a Christian school setting. Why? Because they are ambassadors for Christ using their talents and sphere of influence to make an impact for God. Pray for your child's teachers that God can develop them so that they can effectively teach your child.

POSITIVE ACTIVITIES WITH POSITIVE PEOPLE CAN MAKE A DIFFERENCE

I believe in the potential of extracurricular activities, especially if you have people of faith in positions of leadership. I will always marvel at the team of people Robert Woods has assembled at Cedar Hill High School. Coach Woods has rounded up a group of men of character who have a passion for winning but a greater compulsion to shape the character of the young men in their program. Robert Woods, Paul Phillips, Carlos Linn, and Joey McGuire are all giants in my eyes. No, not physical giants. They are spiritual giants in a world where it is tough to have a deep faith, much less express that faith in a demonstrable way.

Joey McGuire, in particular, has captured my parental respect and admiration. He is a football and powerlifting coach at Cedar Hill High School. He is an outstanding coach. But that is not what I appreciate the most about him. He is also a servant of God making a profound impact on the lives of young men searching for direction every day. He has a deep personal faith that causes him to give the young men under his leadership more than athletic coaching.

I am thankful that he has been in the life of my son because he has encouraged him athletically and, more important, has made a profound impact on him spiritually. For four years he was a positive influence on the physical and spiritual development of my son's life. I will never forget an instance when my son was having a challenge sorting out some things that were going on in his life athletically. Joey McGuire took the extra time to help my son place what was happening in his life in perspective spiritually. On a regular basis, he has gone the extra mile to minister to my son on and off the field. That football coach and teacher has been a gift from God to my son.

Pray that God will place people in your child's life to multiply the instruction and example you provide at home. Pray that God will give your child mentors in his life to help him keep his relationship with Christ in perspective no matter where he is and what he is experiencing.

PRAY FOR A NETWORK OF FAMILY AND FRIENDS

I am a very limited person. That is not a statement of false humility. We all are limited. That is why you need a network of family friends to support you and your parenting. God has made this so abundantly clear throughout our entire life, but especially during the last few years of our lives. You should make this a focus of your prayer life.

God has given us a rich network of family friends who surround our children with all kinds of support. My children have had the luxury of people in their lives over the years who have served as surrogate grandparents, aunts, and uncles. It is dangerous to mention real names because you invariably leave out very important people. I am going to mention a few of their names to illustrate what I am talking about because you should know your network needs to be made up of people with a variety of personalities and skills. This description is not intended to be exhaustive, but hopefully these examples will illustrate the power of a network of family support.

My children have always lived a long way from their extended family, so we have been fortunate enough to have many families like Walter and Mary White, who have been there over the years to support my children during birthdays and special occasions. Walter and Mary's children, Walter Jr. and Danny, are like brothers to my children, who have enjoyed positive Christian fun that has helped mold their character over the years. They have seen what an aunt and uncle would function like through William and Roberta Jones, who have always included our family in their extended family gatherings. They have even had a grandmother away from home in Lois Daniels to remember special days of their lives to supplement the cards and letters they have received from their flesh and blood relatives.

Pray for men in your child's life like our friends Jerry Haynes and Elgin Perkins, who will drop whatever they are doing, and have in the past, to support our family. They have modeled character traits of manhood that complement the example of their father.

And then they need to see neighbors like Lorraine Roberson, who checks on the well-being of their mother almost daily. They will gain so much comfort in knowing that "human angels" like Rita Smith, who sent my wife a personalized e-mail prayer every day for almost an entire year to support her through the initial stages of her bout with breast cancer, exist in the world.

This has been especially important, since we have always lived so far away from our extended family. We have been blessed with a brother and sister-in-law, David and Princess, with their family, who have provided hours of laughter and fun during holiday gatherings and who have brought warmth and pleasure to our lives because they live so close by.

But your children also need to see that distance does not isolate them from a support system. My children saw that in dramatic form when Annie had surgery for her breast cancer. I am sure my children will never forget their aunts Renee and Constance dropping everything in their world to fly miles away from their homes and families to help care for Annie. Nor will my children forget the weekly calls Annie received from her other siblings.

Who takes care of your children when you are not around? Do you have a Jennifer Cox or a Canvas Wesley or a Lynn Owens or a Vornadette Simpson? These are not just names. These are godly people who know our values and make sure our values are promoted in the lives of our children when we can't be there for them.

Can you name a few people who will drop what they are doing to support your children? If not, start praying that God will give you friends who will support your children. I have made this section intensely personal because your child needs a truly personal network to support him. A network of family support and friends will give your children security in a challenging world. Your child needs to know he is not alone in the world.

A MEMBER OF YOUR EXTENDED FAMILY CAN MARK YOUR CHILD'S LIFE

My youngest son wrote the following essay as a part of the application process for college. With his permission I have included this essay to illustrate how powerful the influence of a godly grandfather can be on the life of a child. I was moved by the depth of my son's sincerity. This expression of admiration for his grandfather shows the power of a life well lived on the development of a child. Don't underestimate the power of what God says in Psalm 78.

LIKE ARROWS IN THE HAND OF A WARRIOR . . .

In my short life I have been blessed with the opportunity to be exposed to many different people and situations. One of the people I look up to in this world is my grandfather. He is a great man and a great man of God. He never led the life of a rich man on earth, but there is a great store of treasures awaiting him in heaven. He personifies the man whose "quiver is full," and his children are a blessing to him. There is no doubt in the mind of anyone who knows him or runs across his path that God has done great work through him.

Life is about more than money, and success or achievement can't be measured by such earthly standards. Such is true in the case of my granddaddy. He worked 31 years at the shipyards of Norfolk as a Navy longshoreman. Traveling three hours round trip every morning and evening to work. He worked eight-hour days of backbreaking labor while there. The money he made then would have the average American family of four today complaining and griping. He somehow met the needs of 18 children, and supported his mother for 15+ years as well. Seeing that the money didn't cover all the needs of such a large family, there was a need for some extra support. He obtained that through raising a pen of 50 or more "head of hog" and maintained a large garden of healthy foods and a yard full of chickens. Every August without fail he took the prime pigs to auction and used the proceeds to buy each child new school clothes and pay the tuition of his children who attended college. Sure, it wasn't lobster and steak every night. But I have never heard my mother or aunts and uncles recall receiving anything but wholesome and healthy meals. He did more than nourish their bodies, though. No matter how hard the day was, he always had time to give love and attention to his children. With that love and attention he raised them up in the way that they should go and they did not depart from it.

Being the godly man that he was, his children had no choice but to grow and learn in the knowledge of our Savior. Without fail, on Sunday morning and Wednesday evening the Harvey children would be present at my Great Uncle's church. Not just present, but active members; obviously, with a family that size the children could be the choir. Church was not the only time God was the center of their focus. No one ever sat at Walter Harvey's table and ate without thanking God for providing what was on it, and God was ever-faithful in meeting the needs and even fulfilling some of the wants of this family. The four-bedroom house where he resides and all of his children were raised tells of it. The walls cry out of great memories, and the stove that serves as central heating tells of warm winter evenings drawing the family close. He ruled his house with love and a firm hand, though discipline, I understand, was never a major problem because of the love and respect that existed. Because of that, Walter Harvey's children are successful, contributing members of society and not the statistics it would have been easy for them to become. Through his life, the Scripture becomes real to me when it says, "Like arrows in the hand of a warrior so are the children of one's youth." Now in these trying times when his strength is weak and health is not great, his children are there providing around the clock support. If it's cooking that needs to be done, they do it. A prescription to pick up—it gets picked up. Even outside of the Harvey family his living legacy commands respect.

Proverbs says a good name is of great value. Based on that verse, granddaddy's name is an invaluable asset. Many people know who he is because he offered a helping hand in their time of need. Others know him through the living witness that his children exhibit every day, helping those who can't help themselves and showing other acts of Christian spirit. Everyone knows the class and character that Walter Harvey maintained. He is a trustee at the church of his upbringing and a man who has hidden God's Word in his heart. Though his eyes are betraying him, those Scriptures remain deep in his heart. Even now, though he is more feeble and you must listen closely, he has a wisdom that wells up from deep within. His knowledge comes from life experience and days of attending the school of hard knocks. Even a few weeks ago I went to cut wood for him and we talked for fifteen minutes and I soaked up bits and pieces of life knowledge and insights like a sponge. We talked about relationships, which he knows a little about, considering he has maintained a vibrant marriage (that's single, not plural) for 52 years. We talked about the work ethic, and he knows about that, being the father of 18 kids and feeding them, clothing them, and offering them some of the pleasures in life. And we discussed the importance of education, and in his tired voice he stressed to me that a good education is paramount to being all that I can be. Education coming second only to my continuing growth and knowledge in my relationship with my Lord. Both a good education and an environment conducive to growth I feel I could receive at this college.

Though I see him a few times a year, when we travel to my parent's hometown I would really love to spend a concentrated evening in dialogue and fellowship with my granddaddy. He, along with my father, exemplifies the epitome of a Christian man, father, and husband. If I failed and were half as successful as either of them, I would be well pleased with myself. They are men of God in the truest sense of the words. As iron sharpens iron, so must one Christian man sharpen another. That reason too, would merit spending an evening with Granddaddy.

I had no idea my son had this kind of respect for his grandfather. It is well placed. His grandfather has lived life well before his children, grandchildren, and community. As I reflect back over the years, I wish God had not moved us so far away from my children's grandparents. Yet even with the distance, their grandparents have had a profound impact on the lives of our children.

Little did my son's grandfather know as my son was growing up that there would be a pair of young eyes watching his every move, hanging on every word he spoke. If God has placed godly family members in your child's life, seize the opportunity to benefit from their wisdom.

ENLIST THE SUPPORT OF AS MANY PEOPLE AS POSSIBLE

Expose your children to the people who have "lives worth imitating" as often as you can, while you can. In fact, I would encourage you to seek them out. You never know how God will use other people to help shape your child's character.

FAITH STEPS

1. Do everything you can to make sure your child has a network of friends whose lives exemplify Christian values.

2. Keep your child connected to the community of faith found in your local church.

3. Pray for godly Christian teachers for your child as she develops in her school setting.

4. Give your child the opportunity to have solid Christian mentors in her life.

5. Take advantage of the wonderful experience and maturity that extended family can have on your child's life.

A PARENT'S PRAYER

Father, Thank You that You allow people into our children's lives to help them mature and develop. Please place people in my child's life who love You and will walk alongside my child as she learns to walk with You. Amen.

PARENTING INSIGHTS

SPECIAL CARE INSTRUCTIONS

Research Highlight: Your Child's Safety

Many things that are threats to your child's safety are actually part of your everyday routine. Preventive actions on your part could save you and your child much pain and difficulty.[1]

RESEARCH HIGHLIGHTS

- Take every possible precaution to protect your child from the moment your pregnancy begins. Each year approximately 3 million babies are conceived. Here is what happens to some of them: 500,000 are lost through miscarriages in the first twenty weeks of pregnancy, 24,000 are lost in late miscarriages and stillbirths, 250,000 are born prematurely, and 250,000 are born with birth defects. Many of these problems are the direct result of environmental toxins and other hazards that could be avoided.
- More deaths for children between the ages of one to three are caused by motor vehicle accidents, burns, and suffocation than all the deaths caused by homicide, congenital abnormalities, and cancer combined.
- Although more than 600 children below the age of three were killed in automobile accidents during the last year on record, some 50 percent of those deaths could have been prevented with correct car safety. More than 82 percent of car seats are used incorrectly.
- In 1998, more than 500 children below the age of three years old lost their lives due to suffocation, 400 children under the age of four lost their lives to drowning, 250 lost their lives to burns. Toys caused more than 153,000 serious injuries.
- More than 1 million children have elevated levels of lead in their bodies, which has been proven to increase the risk of disrupted brain development, lowered IQ, and behavior problems.
- Environmental factors such as air pollution, asbestos, lead, mercury,

pesticides, radiation, and solvents and PCBs have been proven to be detrimental to the health, growth, and development of children.

- Cigarette smoking, which in 90 percent of all smokers began in childhood or adolescence, causes more than 350,000 deaths each year.

RESEARCH APPLICATIONS

1. As soon as you discover you are expecting a child, remove as many toxins as possible from your environment to avoid chemically poisoning yourself or your child.
2. Evaluating everything in your house for its potential impact on the safety of your child.
3. Use safety equipment, such as car seats, appropriately.
4. Minimize the accident and injury potential in your environment by doing what you can to lower the incidence of falls, burns, cuts, bites, food poisoning and infections, and other preventable incidents.
5. Stay away from destructive personal habits, such as smoking, that can cause harm to your child.
6. Install fencing and locked gates and take other precautions to protect your child when necessary.
7. Teach your child how to protect himself from dangers in and outside the home.

"The prudent sees the evil and hides himself, But the naïve go on, and are punished for it" (Proverbs 22:3).

Make your child's safety one of your highest parental priorities.

13

WARNING: KEEP AWAY FROM DANGER

Protecting Your Child from Danger

The ship *Andrea Gail* did not know it was going into the "perfect storm."

The crew was so enamored with the worth of the fish they had caught that they lost sight of the danger they faced on the high seas. They ignored the warning signals.

Overconfident, they were facing Hurricane Grace and did not know it.

They were in danger of the high winds, flying debris, and water that was literally overtaking the ship.

Yet they kept going.

By the time they finally turned the ship around, everything was on the brink of being destroyed and it was clear it would be a miracle if they got out of the storm alive.

It was too late.

They ran right into the eye of the storm. The *Andrea Gail* now rests on the bottom of the Bermuda Sea, and the men on that ship rest there as well.

The plot of the movie *The Perfect Storm* is close to the reality facing many homes. Many children are in imminent danger, and their parents are overconfident. There are many dangers lurking around our children that we sometimes underestimate.

Let's hope and pray your family will recognize the danger facing your children and make the necessary adjustments before it is too late to rescue them from the storms of life.

WHAT IS THERE TO FEAR?

God has not given you a spirit of fear. Anytime you are overcome by a spirit of fear, that's a pretty good indication that you are not responding according to the teaching and principles of Scripture. God gives an important insight about fear in Paul's second letter to Timothy. "For God has not given us a spirit of timidity, but of power and love and discipline" (2 Timothy 1:7). When you find yourself allowing fear related to your child to overcome you, meditate on this passage. Seek to draw spiritual lessons from the circumstances you find yourself in. But don't forget that there is a big difference between fear and ignorance.

KNOW YOUR ENEMY

Although you should not have a spirit of fear, you should definitely know your spiritual enemy. Satan is very sophisticated. "Be of sober spirit, be on the alert. Your adversary, the devil, prowls around like a roaring lion, seeking someone to devour" (1 Peter 5:8). He wants you to operate between two extremes. One extreme is a kind of giddy bliss that ignores the fact that there are real dangers you have to watch out for to protect your child. The other extreme is to be so focused on the danger that you miss the presence and power of God.

BE ON THE ALERT

Don't forget that the threat of danger is real. Be on the alert. That means to have a conscious awareness of the things that could sabotage your child's future. Develop a sound grasp of the challenges and obstacles your child faces on a daily basis. Put in place aggressive strategies to protect your child.

Once you develop a clear understanding of the challenges and threats and develop a strategy, trust God to be the ultimate defense of your child's well-being and safety. Strike a balance between exercising the highest levels of responsibility possible and expressing faith in God. Take practical steps to increase your child's capacity to trust God.

WATCH OUT FOR EXCESSIVE STRESS

Stress can be a great enemy to your child's personal growth and success. When your child experiences too much stress it negatively affects his functioning in every area of his life. View excessive stress as a major enemy.

In his book *Stress and Your Child,* Archibald Hart cites statistics that paint a dark picture of the kinds of stressors children face and how that excessive stress can impact a child.[1]

- The suicide rate for adolescents has tripled since 1958, and younger children are killing themselves.
- Children as young as five years old are developing ulcers.
- Researchers have noted an alarming increase in depression in children all across the nation.
- Increasing numbers of younger adolescents and children are turning to alcohol, drugs, sex, and violence, either as an escape from stress or a way of letting off steam.
- Cholesterol levels in children are now skyrocketing, preparing the way for early heart disease.
- Autopsies of children killed in accidents have revealed fatty, fibrous plaque clogging the arteries of fifteen-year-olds and beginning to form in children as young as two or three years of age.
- Accidents are the number one killer of adolescents, and stressed adolescents are two-and-a-half times more likely to have an accident.

Obviously, you couldn't nor would you want to eliminate all stress from your child's life. But try to do a few simple things to decrease excessive stress in your child's life.

- When your child is young, leave him alone to care for himself as little as possible.
- Give your child a home environment that is not characterized by constant conflict and friction among family members (especially parents).
- Provide as much personalized attention as you can. That means less time at work and more time with your child nurturing him at home.
- Create as much routine as possible. Children thrive on the presence of routine.
- Ensure that support is available to deal with challenging school assignments.
- Set clear limits for your child. If you consistently follow the limits, this will be more of a blessing than a burden to your child.

Of course, some of the stress may come from outside the home. Pay attention to that source of stress also.

DON'T IGNORE PEER PRESSURE

One of the greatest sources of stress your child will face is peer pressure. The desire to be accepted by children his own age is so great that your child will be tempted to make some decisions that will be totally out of line with what you have taught him and not in his best interest. You can't ignore the reality of peer pressure, no matter how effectively you teach your children.

This was dramatically illustrated to me when I served as program director of a juvenile placement facility for delinquent boys and girls. I will never forget the weekend one of the girls who had been a model student for months ran away from the facility. Everyone was baffled. It was going to be just a matter of weeks before she would be free to go home to be with her family. She had made dramatic improvement over the months she had been there. Yet for no apparent reason she ran away.

When Sylvia (name changed) came back from her runaway weekend, her words were shocking. When she was asked by the staff why she had run away, she responded, "I went off campus to have sex. All the other girls on the unit said they were not virgins, and something was wrong with me because I was. Now I am OK."

What a tragedy! Peer pressure caused this young girl to give up her virginity and imminent freedom. Sometimes peer pressure can cause your child to be drawn into self-destructive habits and inappropriate sexual practices.

GIVE THEM A BIBLICAL VIEW OF THEIR SEXUALITY

A prime example of how you can help your child is to give him the biblical instruction and personal guidance he needs to develop godly character in the area of sexuality. Most children gain their sex education from a lot of places other than their parents. A recent survey by the Kaiser Foundation gives some very interesting results about where teenagers receive the greatest amount of information on sex:

- 61% Peers
- 44% Sex-education classes
- 40% TV and movies
- 39% Teen magazines
- 32% Parents[2]

You need to work hard to make sure you are the main instructor in the area of sex education for your child. There is some good news about this responsibility if you take it seriously. A 1999 report by the Annie E. Casey foundation reveals that one out of two teenagers say they trust their parents most for reliable and complete information on sex.[3] You just need to gain the courage and confidence to talk about sexuality with your children.

It should be encouraging to you to know that teenagers gain a greater deal of insight and courage when they receive positive instruction from parents than they do from any other source of instruction. The National Campaign to Prevent Teen Pregnancy: Project Reality found that "93% of teens felt it is important for teens to be given a strong message about sexual abstinence."[4]

Where do you get the insight to communicate the foundational truths your children need to understand? Well, the Bible has a lot to say about this important area. A central passage that communicates the heart of God on this subject is found in Paul's first letter to the church at Thessalonica.

> For this is the will of God, your sanctification; that is, that you abstain from sexual immorality; that each of you know how to possess his own vessel in sanctification and honor, not in lustful passion, like the Gentiles who do not know God; and that no man transgress and defraud his brother in the matter because the Lord is the avenger in all these things, just as we also told you before and solemnly warned you. For God has not called us for the purpose of impurity, but in sanctification. (1 Thessalonians 4:3–7)

Remind your children how beautiful their sexuality is. It is a gift from God to them as an expression of His love for each one of us. But it is so beautiful, it is best enjoyed in the context of a marriage relationship between a husband and wife.

There are plenty of object lessons you can use from the culture to help your children understand their sexuality. Ruth Senter communicates the importance of a child guarding their virginity with this powerful poem:

FRAGILE: HANDLE WITH CARE

There's a beautiful gift inside this package.
It's wrapped for protection,
Tied for security.
Stamped: "Fragile!"
"Handle with Care!"
It's easy to loosen the strings,
To let anyone tear away
The wrapping,
To give the gift without commitment—
Offer it to the highest bidder,
Or hand it out as the prize
for a game.
There is a gift wrapped inside this brown paper.
It's for keeps—
Not to be exchanged.
No deposit. Non-returnable.
It's a surprise,
A happy treat to be opened by the person
To whom it's addressed,
On the date marked "Forever."

—Ruth Senter

That means you must give your children clear instructions and boundaries concerning God's perspective of their sexuality. Here are a few suggestions.

- Expose your children to some simple but clear verses of Scripture that teach about sexuality.
- Pick up age-appropriate books, tapes, and other resources that give a clear biblical overview of sexuality to supplement the values and principles communicated in the Scripture.
- Engage in frank, open conversations with your children to help them understand the beauty of their sexuality.
- Give regular critiques of the kinds of false pictures of sexuality portrayed in the media.

Unfortunately, sexual addiction is not the only danger your child could potentially face.

TEACH YOUR CHILD THE DANGER OF ADDICTIVE SUBSTANCES

Yes. We still have a serious problem with substances that cause addictive behavior, such as drugs, alcohol, and tobacco. Be on the alert. We will use alcohol as an example.

Jerry Johnston points out some startling statistics in his book *It's Killing Our Kids: The Growing Epidemic of Teenage Alcohol Abuse and Addiction.*

- Every day, Americans consume 15.7 million gallons of beer and ale, equivalent to 28 million six-packs—enough cans to fill a stadium 30 feet deep.
- Every 24 hours, Americans consume 1.2 million gallons of hard liquor, enough to get 26 million people thoroughly drunk.
- The Centers for Disease Control (CDC) report there are more than 100,000 alcohol-related deaths a year due to, among other things, diseases like cirrhosis of the liver . . .
- The American Hospital Association reports that half of all hospital admissions are alcohol related.

- The National Safety Council's 1989 Accident Facts asserts the apocalyptic fact that every twenty-seven minutes a person dies in an alcohol-related crash.
- Each year at least 24,000 people are killed in alcohol-related tragedies.[5]

Let me stop there. More chilling statistics could be listed, but the point is made. Alcohol is a threat to your child's health, safety, and even life. The anonymous poem below focuses on the dangers of heroin, but it could apply to all forms of drugs, alcohol, and addictive behavior.

> King Heroin is my shepherd, I shall not want,
> He maketh me lie down in the gutters.
> He leadeth me beside the troubled waters.
> He destroyeth my soul.

Your actions and attitudes will have a profound impact on your child's behavior. Here are some suggestions.

- Practice what you preach; watch your own habits.
- Keep things out of your home you don't want your children to indulge in.
- Educate your children to the dangers of drugs and other addictive substances.
- Find positive, wholesome alternatives to negative forms of pleasure.

BE ALERT TO THE DANGERS AND BENEFITS OF THE INTERNET

The Internet is a wonderful resource. It is a medium that can connect your child with information, places, people, and experiences twenty-four hours a day. That is a wonderful reality. But the Internet also has the potential of great danger for your child. Improperly used, it can be a dangerous tool in the hands of people who don't have your child's best interests at heart. That is why you have to be informed and wise about the Internet.

Here are a few practical suggestions to minimize the impact of unintended consequences your child will experience while taking advantage of the wonderful resources available on the Internet.

- Place an Internet filter on your computer to block out unwanted images and information.
- Set limits on the amount of time your child can spend on the Internet each day.
- Discuss the specific expectations you have for the way the computer will be used in your home and give clear guidelines on what is inappropriate.
- Keep your child out of unwholesome chat rooms.
- Warn your child about the "stranger danger" present on the Internet.

With all these warnings, you could easily get the impression the Internet is inherently bad. It does not have to be. With the right guidelines and instruction, it can be a wonderful resource for your child and family.

BE AWARE OF VIOLENT TELEVISION, MOVIES, AND VIDEOS

If television, movies, and videos were ever something you needed to watch carefully as a parent, it is now. These three media are having a profound influence on the intellectual and emotional growth of children. You definitely need to think carefully about how you use these media in your home.

Television is a pervasive influence in our culture

Violence on television is a real force to contend with if you are serious about protecting the spiritual and emotional vitality of your child. A recent study pointed out that the average child will watch more than 16,000 murders and 200,000 acts of violence before he reaches the age of eighteen. A child will see half that amount of violence by the time he completes elementary school.[6]

In case you don't think this makes any difference, let me point you to two studies cited in *The Christian Educator's Handbook on Family Life Education.*

> The impact on behavior is predictable. Two prominent Surgeon General reports in the last two decades link violence on television and aggressive be-

> havior in children and teenagers. In addition, the National Institute of Mental Health issued a ninety-four page report entitled, "Television and Behavior: Ten Years of Scientific Progress and Implications for the Eighties." They found "overwhelming scientific evidence that 'excessive' violence on television spills over into the playground and the streets. . . ." Long-term studies are even more disturbing. University of Illinois psychologist Leonard Eron studied children at age eight and then again at age eighteen. He found that television habits established at the age of eight influenced aggressive behavior throughout childhood and adolescent years. The more violent the program preferred by the boys in the third grade, the more aggressive their behavior, both at that time and ten years later. He therefore concluded that "the effects of television violence on aggression [are] cumulative."[7]

Do your child's television viewing habits matter? You bet they do! That's why it is important you take this area very seriously.

Movies are also a place to keep your antennae up

A recent Gallup poll indicated that 40 percent of Americans think we should pay special attention to the amount of violence present in movies. Let me cite an example referred to in *The Christian Educator's Handbook on Family Life Education.*

> We are a very sick society judging by the latest fare of violence in the movies. The body count is staggering: 32 people killed in the *RoboCop* and 81 killed in the sequel; 264 are killed in *Die Hard 2;* and the film *Silence of the Lambs* deals with a psychopath who murders women and skins them.[8]

Don't take anything for granted with the movies you allow your children to watch. Be aware and make wise choices.

Videos can influence your child's behavior and values in a significant way

Just in case you think videos don't influence your child, let me alert you to a few facts you should consider. In her book *A Parent's Guide to the Best Children's Videos and Where to Find Them,* Mary Turck did a great job of identifying some of the key issues. "Sex, violence, and language are among the most frequently mentioned concerns about children's video and television viewing. They are not the only issues—roles of men and women, race and religion, values, manners, prejudices, and politics all come in for consideration by various parents."[9]

The big idea is that there is no such thing as an unimportant viewing experience. Every viewing experience communicates something to your child. You should be aware of what's going on so that you can make sure it matches your values and vision for the growth and development of your child.

Here are some practical suggestions to protect your child from the dangers of television, movies, and violent videos.

- Set limits on the amount of time your child watches television every day.
- Limit his television and movie viewing to programs that will contribute to his growth and maturity.
- Restrict your child's movie viewing habits to entertainment that does not promote violence or other values that are inconsistent with your standards as a family.
- Encourage your child to engage in active recreational activities that cause him to think and move rather than be engaged in a passive activity like television.
- Get out and do things with your child to stimulate his creativity and encourage him to learn to enjoy positive activities.

KNOW ABOUT MUSIC THAT CAN MOVE YOUR CHILDREN AWAY FROM GOD

Music is a powerful medium. When properly used, it can relax, enhance learning, and communicate important ideas. But the opposite is also true. When it is not used properly, it can distract, distort, and develop faulty patterns of thought in the heart of your child.

- Teach your child the power of music to influence his thoughts and behavior.
- Give your child the skills he needs to discriminate between wholesome and negative music.

- Expose your child to all types of music.
- Keep a variety of music on hand in your home so your child can learn how to make positive musical selections at home with your guidance.
- Refuse to allow your child to play music that attacks Christian values in your home.
- Don't "throw out the baby with the bath water." Let your child enjoy good music.

Help your child develop an appetite for listening to music that is entertaining and cultivates their walk with God. Bryan Belknap offers a brief but clear definition of Christian music that may be helpful to you as a focus point to direct your child's interest in music. Encourage your child to listen to "any music in any style that supports a biblical worldview and brings listeners—both believers and nonbelievers—closer to Christ. It's music that prompts our Creator to say, 'Well done.'"

That's the kind of music you ultimately want your children to fall in love with.

BE AWARE OF DANGEROUS PEOPLE

As I am sure you know, every person your child comes in contact with does not have his best interests at heart. Sometimes children operate with naïve assumptions about the people they come in contact with. Use wisdom and carefully help your child understand that.

Recent estimates indicate that between two hundred and three hundred stranger abductions occur across the United States each year. The estimates also indicate that as many as 20 percent of girls and 7 percent of boys will not reach the age of eighteen without experiencing some form of sexual abuse.[10] What should you do?

- Don't leave your child without appropriate adult supervision.
- Teach your child the limits of appropriate contact other adults should have with him.
- Instruct your child how to ask for help if he feels like he is in danger.
- Show your child how to escape from situations and circumstances when he feels threatened.

- Take the time to make sure your child has proper identification on him at all times.

KNOW YOUR LIMITATIONS

Here is where I have to make a sobering statement. After you have done all these things, accept the fact that the older your child, the more your control over the people they are exposed to and the danger they face will decrease. That forces you back to the posture of faith and trust in God.

You also need to give your child the capacity to accept God's sovereign control over his life. It means that sometimes neither we, nor our children, will be able to understand everything God is doing. In other words, you can't do enough to guarantee the safety of your children. Ultimately, God wants us to reach a position of faith and trust that releases us to resolve that whatever God wills we are willing and able to accept.

That posture only comes when our ultimate passion is to please and serve Him. Cassie Bernall was, from a human perspective, an unfortunate victim of the shootings at Columbine High School in Littleton, Colorado. But her life did not end in vain. Her testimony gives us—and the parents and teachers of our children—a model of how to approach the dangers of life. An article in the *Baptist Bulletin* cited a poem she wrote that first appeared in the *Boston Globe* just days after her death.

May the poem Cassie penned just prior to her death give you a perspective that will complement all the steps you take to protect your child and shape his perspective about the dangers of this world we all live in.

According to the *Boston Globe,* Cassie Bernall's brother found this poem. She had written it just two days prior to April 20, the day of her death:

Now I have given up on everything else
I have found it to be the only way
To really know Christ and to experience
The mighty power that brought Him back to life again, and to find
Out what it means to suffer and to
Die with Him. So, whatever it takes
I will be one who lives in the fresh
Newness of life of those who are
Alive from the dead.[11]

FAITH STEPS

1. Determine to replace fear with a conscious commitment to do everything possible to provide for your child's safety and protection.

2. Equip your child to recognize and escape from people, situations, media, and events that could jeopardize his well-being.

3. Provide a wholesome and safe environment to foster your child's growth and maturity.

4. Teach and model for your child the biblical view of his sexuality.

5. Give your child the confidence he needs to trust God to accomplish His will for his life and protect him from anything that would block God's purposes.

A PARENT'S PRAYER

Father, Thank You that You have not given me a spirit of fear and dread. Help me recognize people, situations, and events that could endanger my child. Give me the wisdom to place barriers and boundaries in my child's life to help protect him. Guide me so that I can teach my child to exercise godly wisdom in his everyday decisions and relationships. Amen.

PARENTING INSIGHTS

S P E C I A L C A R E I N S T R U C T I O N S

Research Highlight: Childhood and Violence

Unfortunately, violence is a phenomenon many children will have to grapple with beginning early in their childhood and throughout their adolescent development. Children are consistently exposed to violence through television, video games, interaction at schools, and potentially in their community if it is characterized by frequent violent behavior. Research demonstrates that exposure to violence contributes to later violent behavior, a callousness toward the negative impact of violence, a fear of being a victim, and sometimes attraction to the rewards that appear to follow violence.[12]

RESEARCH HIGHLIGHTS

- Before they reach the age of eighteen, one in five kids will commit a violent act.
- Children see 8,000 murders and 100,000 other violent acts on television by the time they complete the elementary grades.
- Current trends point to an increase in violent arrest rates among juveniles of more than a 20 percent increase by the year 2010.
- Adults are three times less likely to be victimized by violence than teens.

Most research points to several consistent contributors to violence among children and teenagers including poverty, gang affiliation, substance abuse, witnessing violence, and long-term exposure to violence in their personal environment.

RESEARCH APPLICATIONS

1. Let your kids see you solving problems in a nonviolent way as a routine of life.

2. As much as possible, direct your child away from friends and peers who use violence to solve problems.
3. Carefully monitor the amount of violence your child is exposed to in movies, on television, or as he plays video games.
4. Equip your child with specific problem-solving skills to use in the challenging situations he may encounter.
5. Develop relationships with your child's friends so you can give him personal advice and counsel in this area of his life.
6. If your child is of legal age to possess firearms, make sure he follows all the safety rules and is trained to care for and use them properly.
7. Provide your child with positive entertaining alternatives to using his time engaging in activities that directly or indirectly promote violence.

"He who is slow to anger is better than the mighty, and he who rules his spirit, than he who captures a city" (Proverbs 16:32).

Teach your children to avoid violence personally and interpersonally as much as they possibly can.

14

TROUBLESHOOTING

Discipline from a Biblical Perspective

Far too many times I have seen the classic parent-child standoff. The parent is standing in a show of control over a sitting child. The child has his arms folded defiantly. His face screams out the challenge, "I am sitting down on the outside, but standing up on the inside." In other words, my heart is in rebellion while my body obeys. That is not the goal of biblical discipline.

BIBLICAL DISCIPLINE HAS THE GOAL OF SHAPING THE CHILD'S HEART

Biblical discipline changes the heart as well as the actions of the child. Discipline involves changing behavior, but it starts with cultivating righteousness in the heart. You can have a child who displays correct behavior on the outside but has a heart that is defiant toward God.

Unfortunately, many parents sometimes confuse conformity in outward behavior with inward character transformation. Getting a child to conform and obey parental instructions is sometimes very difficult. Helping a child to have a pure heart in the process of being disciplined is even more challenging.

BIBLICAL DISCIPLINE TAKES HARD WORK

Discipline doesn't come naturally like the native flowers of Texas. Texas is known for beautiful, colorful natural flowers. They are planted once in a particular area of the state, and it seems every year after that they reappear without cultivation. God has made these beautiful flowers to need only a minimal amount of human cultivation. It is incredible.

Unlike the grasses of Texas, discipline in the life of a child does not naturally happen; it has to be cultivated by human involvement. The cultivation of discipline in the life of a child is intentional, not accidental. It happens by careful parental choice, not random chance. But that may raise a very natural question. Why should we place so much emphasis on discipline?

BIBLICAL DISCIPLINE IS BUILT ON A FOUNDATION OF LOVE

God's love for us is clearly demonstrated by His willingness to discipline us as believers. God's Word offers us a perfect example of the cultivation process. The best model of cultivating righteousness is the work of God in our lives. Hebrews 12:4–13 offers us a snapshot of God's approach to discipline.

> You have not yet resisted to the point of shedding blood in your striving against sin; and you have forgotten the exhortation which is addressed to you as sons,
>
> "My son, do not regard lightly the discipline of the Lord,
> Nor faint when you are reproved by Him;
> For those whom the Lord loves He disciplines,
> And He scourges every son whom He receives."
>
> It is for discipline that you endure; God deals with you as with sons; for what son is there whom his father does not discipline? But if you are without dis-

> cipline, of which all have become partakers, then you are illegitimate children and not sons. Furthermore, we had earthly fathers to discipline us, and we respected them; shall we not much rather be subject to the Father of spirits, and live? (Hebrews 12:4–9)

In the same way, parental love often expresses it itself in godly discipline.

BIBLICAL DISCIPLINE IS CHILD CENTERED WITH A LONG-RANGE GOAL

A parent who fails to discipline his child sometimes reveals that he loves personal peace and tranquility more than the child who desperately cries out for discipline. We can sometimes overlook problems with our children that require extraordinary amounts of time to resolve. That calls for a special effort on our part as parents.

I remember addressing a persistent problem with one of my children. We were in an apparent standoff. I canceled my appointments for a couple of days, knowing this problem would arise. When the problem surfaced, I sat down with my child, looked him in the eye, and said, "I have the time. I am not leaving until we work this out." That response set the tone for how the household would respond to later problems.

BIBLICAL DISCIPLINE IS LAID ON A FOUNDATION OF KNOWLEDGE BASED ON PARENTAL INSTRUCTION

Following the passage from the book of Hebrews just quoted, the author continues:

> For [our fathers] disciplined us for a short time as seemed best to them, but [God] disciplines us for our good, so that we may share His holiness. All discipline for the moment seems not to be joyful, but sorrowful; yet to those who have been trained by it, afterwards it yields the peaceful fruit of righteousness. (Hebrews 12:10–11)

The goal of all parental instruction is to cultivate righteous behavior in the life of the child. If a parent has the right focus as he administers discipline, it will always be proactive rather than reactive. A number of truths and principles found in the Ten Commandments and other sections of Scripture give a solid framework for cultivating righteousness in the life of children. Appropriate parental discipline will be directed toward the child's developing character that honors God based on the foundational teachings of Scripture (Ephesians 6:4).

You can be proactive about the process of discipline by teaching your children these principles as part of the routine of your family experience. The structure for this teaching comes from the book of Exodus in the listing of the Ten Commandments.

Respect for God. Make sure your child has a healthy respect for God. Biblical discipline has as part of its foundation keeping your child properly focused on giving God the honor and respect He is due. You should first model a healthy respect for God. This respect is also illustrated by the reverence we give to the name of God.

> "I am the Lord your God, who brought you out of the land of Egypt, out of the house of slavery. . . . You shall not take the name of the Lord your God in vain, for the Lord will not leave him unpunished who takes His name in vain." (Exodus 20:2, 7)

Be careful not to use the name of the Lord in vain, and teach your children to follow your example.

Proper regard for material possessions or artificial objects of worship. Help your children maintain a biblical approach toward how they handle their possessions. Our natural human tendency is to place more emphasis than we should on the importance of material possessions and artificial objects of worship. Godly parental instruction presents a balanced perspective for children on how to handle things. You have an awesome opportunity to let your children see a proper attitude toward material possessions. When you see your child elevating things and/or artificial objects of worship to a place of authority in her life, aggressively correct it.

> "You shall have no other gods before Me. You shall not make for yourself an idol, or any likeness of what is in heaven above or on the earth

> beneath or in the water under the earth. You shall not worship them or serve them; for I, the Lord your God, am a jealous God, visiting the iniquity of fathers on the children, on the third and the fourth generations of those who hate Me, but showing lovingkindness to thousands, to those who love Me and keep My commandments." (Exodus 20:3–6)

Balance in personal activity. Teach your child to keep work in its proper place in her personal routine. God places a high premium on each person maintaining personal balance.

One of the ways we can demonstrate to our children recognition of the importance of balance is the amount of time *we* give to rest. Helping children get this area right as they grow up in our homes is one of the most important gifts we can give them. Scripture uses this as a test of our trust and dependence on God rather than on our abilities.

> "Remember the sabbath day, to keep it holy. Six days you shall labor and do all your work, but the seventh day is a sabbath of the Lord your God; in it you shall not do any work, you or your son or your daughter, your male or female servant or your cattle or your sojourner who stays with you. For in six days the Lord made the heavens and the earth, the sea and all that is in them, and rested on the seventh day; therefore the Lord blessed the sabbath day and made it holy." (Exodus 20:8–11)

You can learn a lot from the principle of the Sabbath given to the people of God about the importance of keeping our work in proper perspective. The life of a minister can make this especially challenging, but no one is exempt from this important responsibility. What a great opportunity to let our children see this modeled in our lives from an early age (Exodus 20:9–11).

Respect for parents. Don't compromise on your expectation that your child respects your role as her parent. This principle is so important that God connects it to the length of our lives. The home offers an environment for children to learn to respect all forms of divine authority based on the level of respect shown for parents. Many children don't know how to respect church leaders, teachers, law enforcement officers, and other community authorities because they never learned respect in their homes.

"Honor your father and your mother, that your days may be prolonged in the land which the Lord your God gives you." (Exodus 20:12)

In my days as a superintendent of a juvenile facility, it was a very common experience to see that the children who had the hardest time responding to the authority of the staff were the ones who were shamelessly disrespectful to their parents. Make this respect for all legitimate authority, especially yours, an important part of your household standards. You will never regret it.

Respect for life. Give your child a deep respect for human life. God is the creator of life. Life is sacred to God. Parents have an important responsibility to teach children to value life. Unfortunately, our society has adopted some socially approved practices that compromise on this important value. You have the opportunity to establish and maintain God's perspective in your home.

"You shall not murder." (Exodus 20:13)

From the earliest moments of your child's life, help her understand that *all* human life is sacred to God. Model this conviction by the way you respond to people of all ages, ethnic groups, economic levels, and educational backgrounds. Don't discriminate based on any of these external characteristics. Your example will serve your child well when she has to make important life decisions.

Respect for sexual purity. Be your child's first instructor about her sexuality. God's Word clearly states that sex was created by God for the sanctity of the marriage relationship between a man and his wife. Sex is a wonderful gift from God. It is so wonderful that our children need to understand that it needs to be protected and treasured.

Failure to talk openly about sexuality with children when they are young increases the likelihood of their promiscuity as adolescents. In spite of the research that demonstrates the value of such conversations, parents don't spend enough time talking openly with their children about sexual issues. Be careful to speak to them on their level and only address the issues they can understand. Don't assume their curiosity about this important area is a problem.

I remember vividly an instance where my response to a question one of my sons asked at a very early age was based on some faulty assumptions. Annie and I were riding along in the car talking while my son was sitting in the back seat. All of a sudden he asked a question about sexuality that revealed a level of knowledge we didn't even dream he had at that age. We had talked very openly about sex, but not on the level of his question. Although he never knew it, we both were pretty shocked. I proceeded to answer his question with a deep physiological answer because I thought he knew more than he really did and needed an answer to match his knowledge.

Then I turned around to ask him how he learned so much detail about sex. I saw that he had a set of headphones on and was listening to a tape player. When I reached back to look at the tape in the player it became clear he was listening, innocently, to a message I had given previously in a church setting on "Biblical Sexuality."

Ah! Now I understood why he was asking that question and realized that my response was far more than he needed or had the capacity to understand. I restated my answer with about a seven-word response. He said, "OK," and picked up his book and read with peace of mind.

Whew! I turned around and kept talking to Annie with a *real* peace of mind. Lesson learned. Make sure you understand what your child understands and continually help her grow in knowledge as she matures and develops.

Share with your child that any pattern of sexual conduct outside of what the Scripture teaches is outside of the will of God.

> "You shall not commit adultery." (Exodus 20:14)

Unfortunately, we live in a world that, through media and music, sometimes promotes "free sex" without consequences. That is even more of a reason why you should be absolutely clear with your children about why God created sex.

Respect for the property of others. Teach your child to respect the property of others. Taking something that belongs to another person is wrong. Biblical parenting assumes the role of shaping the values and the conscience of children so that they understand the importance of respecting the property rights of other people.

> "You shall not steal." (Exodus 20:15)

Pay careful attention to small habits that send large messages about your character to your child.

Respect for honesty in communication. Avoid saying things about people that are untrue. The Scripture places a high premium on integrity of speech.

Set boundaries for your child with respect to what she says about other people. Help her develop the practice of speaking with integrity in your home environment.

> "You shall not bear false witness against your neighbor." (Exodus 20:16)

Cultivate this important personal trait through communication with siblings and in other interpersonal relationships.

Respect for the provision of God. The Bible gives a strong warning against covetousness. Children can very easily fall into the trap of comparing themselves to other children in terms of what they have.

> "You shall not covet your neighbor's house; you shall not covet your neighbor's wife or his male servant or his female servant or his ox or his donkey or anything that belongs to your neighbor." (Exodus 20:17)

This can lead to an unhealthy preoccupation with wanting more things and unhealthy relationships. In essence, it could result in dissatisfaction with God's provision. Remind your child every day of how fortunate she is to have what God has given her. Help her to learn the important quality of contentment.

There are many other truths communicated through Scripture as a part of the "instruction of the Lord." These examples of parental instruction illustrate that discipline properly administered has the potential to achieve its goal of nurturing godliness in the lives of our children. If a parent engages in positive discipline, it should be positive in orientation, not negative. Sometimes it has to be presented in a punitive mode, but that should not be the norm in biblical parenting.

BIBLICAL DISCIPLINE NURTURES THE PERSON

Discipline is much more than achieving a particular behaviorial goal. The beauty of biblical discipline is that it communicates the idea of instruction and cultivation of character so that the child experiences strength and character. The book of Hebrews says: "Therefore, strengthen the hands that are weak and the knees that are feeble, and make straight paths for your feet, so that the limb which is lame may not be put out of joint, but rather be healed" (Hebrews 12:12–13).

God's pattern of discipline always produces a stronger person after the process is complete. And discipline does involve a process. The process involves much more than simple obedience; rather, it helps bring out a person who is more mature and is stronger as a believer.

PROACTIVE DISCIPLINE: ADMINISTER WITH WISDOM

There are practical steps you can take to make sure your choices are best for your child. It will always be best if you can be proactive when disciplining your children. Be positive. There are a lot of things you can do to cultivate righteous behavior in your child's life before a problem occurs.

1. *Freedom endowment.* Give your child the sense that you trust her by giving her as much freedom as her maturity can handle to make choices.
2. *Affirmation touch.* A gentle touch on your child's shoulder when she displays responsible behavior can be a great motivator and source of encouragement.
3. *Lessons from life experiences.* Capture as many lessons as possible from your child's spontaneous life experiences as possible. Teach spon-

taneously. Teach her as you see her grappling with her daily choices. Turn life activities into a positive classroom for personal maturity.

4. *Verbal praise.* Liberally affirm her verbally for her positive characteristics and actions that honor God.
5. *Life situational exercises.* Place your child in situations that will allow her to develop important skills. Tell her the behavior you want her to display, with the rewards and consequences explained clearly.
6. *Responsibility checks.* Before major problems occur, give your child continuous feedback about the level of responsibility she is demonstrating. Don't wait for a major crisis before you give her feedback.
7. *Removal of distractions.* Eliminate as many things as possible that can distract your child. If you see that things like television, toys, and other peers are contributing to misbehavior in your child, direct her to use her time and energy in other ways.

REACTIVE DISCIPLINE: ADMINISTER WITH GRACE AND SENSITIVITY

No matter how creative you are, your child will make poor choices from time to time. Here are some strategies you may find effective in your effort to help your child develop solid character.

1. *Conviction clarification.* When your child makes a poor choice, review her motivations with her. If the choice is clearly a case of negative intent, then use the situation as a teaching opportunity to refocus her value system in a correct direction.
2. *Verbal rebuke.* Don't be too harsh, but use words that clearly communicate your thoughts about her behavior. Focus your words on the child's behavior, not on her person.
3. *Loss of privileges.* In many cases, you can help your child overcome misbehavior by temporarily removing her freedom to engage in activities she enjoys: taking away her toys, placing her in a position to think more carefully about her actions (as in a "time-out").
4. *Expanded responsibility.* When your child has not appropriately handled assignments or time you have given, you may find it helpful to reassign the previous responsibility or give her expanded responsibilities to help her develop the self-discipline she needs.

5. *Reconciliation.* When your child has problems with interpersonal relationships, focus your disciplinary actions on the way she deals with conflicts. Insist that she attempt to make amends with the sibling or other person she is in conflict with.
6. *Restitution.* If your child's misbehavior caused a loss to someone else, the child should make restitution. This will be a great way to teach her the value of the property of others.
7. *Punishment.* Punishment should be the discipline technique of last resort and therefore very rarely used.

You should be intentional about your decisions. Don't let your emotions dictate your actions. Choose the discipline technique that will be most helpful in the cultivating righteousness in the life of your child.

PRACTICE THE SEVEN B'S OF DISCIPLINE

As you help your child develop a lifestyle that honors God, the suggestions below will help you keep her needs as your highest priority. You will fail from time to time. But if you focus on her needs, God will help you reflect His character and love in all that you do.

Be clear

Make your expectations clear to your child. Sometimes we assume our children understand what we want them to do, and they often don't because we speak in our language instead of theirs. When you sense your child is having a hard time obeying you, stop and think if your instructions and expectations were clear.

Be in control

Don't administer reactive discipline when you are angry. You could say or do something hurtful to your child. If you feel your emotions are boiling over, stop! Take the time to compose yourself before you attempt to deal with your child's misbehavior.

Be calm

Keep your voice down and your tone on a level that promotes harmony. If you are calm in the way you address your child's misbehavior, she is much more likely to learn from the discipline you choose to give.

Be consistent

Don't make discipline decisions based on your desire to impress others or for convenience. Avoid the "public angel, private brat syndrome." This syndrome can cause you to be inconsistent if you are not careful. You may be tempted to not administer discipline when nobody sees your child's misbehavior and respond if your child embarrasses you. Always make decisions based on what is best for your child.

Be committed

Sometimes it will be very difficult to discipline your child because you are tired of dealing with problems. You will be tempted to just ignore her misbehavior. As hard as it may be, you still need to show your love for her by providing the careful blend of encouragement, confrontation, and accountability that is needed.

Be considerate

Your child has feelings and needs for you to remember that when you are responding to misbehavior. Try to avoid embarrassing her unless you believe it is absolutely necessary. Follow this simple rule: Treat your child the way you would want to be treated in a similar situation.

Be compassionate

God gives us a wonderful model. He doesn't give us the full weight of the consequences we deserve. He is merciful. What a great model! Your child needs tenderness and mercy as she grows and develops into adult maturity.

Your attitude is an important element of the discipline process. Practicing these "B's of Discipline" is a simple decision you can make about your response to your child's misbehavior that will keep your discipline positive and nurturing.

THEY DON'T ALWAYS UNDERSTAND

As we discipline our children, it is important for us to keep in mind that our overriding goal has to be to make them stronger and more stable rather than just more compliant.

We have learned much from our children. Gracie, my lovely youngest daughter, has experienced a great deal of physical pain during her young life. She has spent her fair share of time in the doctor's office. During her first few years of life she was hospitalized more than six separate times.

We learned a lot during those days about God, family, and ourselves. Through her experience I also learned a little bit more about ministry as a father. On one of those occasional hospital stays, the nurses had to draw blood from Gracie and needed to insert an IV into her arm. For some reason, that simple routine was sometimes a challenging exercise. It seemed every available hospital staff person was involved in helping.

Then, knowing that I had a calming effect on Gracie, the nurse asked me to come over and hold Gracie down while a couple of the nurses held her and inserted the needle.

I will never forget Gracie's words and plaintive stare.

Her soft brown eyes met mine and her words echoed throughout the room. "No, Daddy, no." It was clear to me that my actions were motivated by love and intended to foster my daughter's best interests. I was using my stature and strength to nurture her so she could be healthy and strong.

That was not how she saw it at that moment.

But I became convinced that my ministry to her was sometimes most significant at the times when she least recognized and appreciated it. The control I exerted over her little body was so that she could be healthy and whole.

Discipline involves providing the nurture and controls a child needs to reach her full potential, even if sometimes she doesn't understand or appreciate it.

FAITH STEPS

1. Clearly establish God's standard as the ultimate guide for your household.

2. Create a clear set of expectations with rewards and consequences.

3. View the process of disciplining your children as cultivating righteousness rather than demanding conformity.

4. Expect children to display their humanity as a part of their human experience.

5. Be patient. Making a masterpiece takes time. Cultivating righteousness will also take time.

A PARENT'S PRAYER

Lord, Help me to model for my child a life of holiness and then may the life I live inspire her to obey You. Help me teach my child how to love You and with all her heart display righteousness through her daily actions. When she makes mistakes, and I know she will, keep my heart calm so that I can correct her with grace and sensitivity. May I respond to her failures with the same measure of mercy that You extend to me. Amen.

PARENTING INSIGHTS

SPECIAL CARE INSTRUCTIONS

Research Highlight: The Danger of Family and Child Abuse and Neglect

Family abuse can be spousal abuse or abuse of a child at the hand of her parents. The National Center and Clearinghouse for Abuse and Neglect says, "Child is a person who has not attained the lesser of: [1] The age of 18 [2] Except in cases of sexual abuse, the age specified by the child protection law of the State in which the child resides. Child abuse and neglect is, at a minimum: Any recent act or failure to act on the part of a parent or caretaker which results in death, serious physical or emotional harm, sexual abuse or exploitation [or an] act or failure to act which presents an imminent risk of serious harm."[1]

RESEARCH HIGHLIGHTS

- Some 1 to 4 million people per year are abused by people they would consider intimates; 30 percent of female murder victims in the U.S. are slain by husbands or boyfriends (U.S. Department of Justice). More than half of the men who assault their wives also abuse their children; child abuse is 15 times more likely to occur in homes where domestic violence is present.
- One study found that the only difference between delinquent and nondelinquent youth was the presence of a history of family violence or abuse against the delinquent youth.
- Child abuse often occurs when parents have not learned how to deal with anger and frustration in a nondestructive manner, are addicted to alcohol or other substances, or are experiencing a great deal of external pressure, such as illness or financial problems.
- Of some 2,806,000 referrals in 1998, more than 900,000 children were found to be victims of abuse and neglect and that resulted in 1,100 deaths.[2] The highest victimization rate was for children from birth to three years old.

- Some 1,397,000 children in the U.S. (20 of every 1,000 children in the population) received preventive services. These services helped parents of children at risk understand a child's developmental stages and give them important parenting skills.

RESEARCH APPLICATIONS

1. Solve interpersonal conflicts with your spouse nonviolently. Avoid using destructive words with your mate so that your child sees appropriate ways to express personal frustration; if you have extreme difficulty in this area, seek help.
2. Focus your actions and words toward building up your child and helping her to fulfill her God-given potential.
3. Stay away from substances, practices, or influences that can distort your judgment as you respond to your child. Never administer discipline to your child when you are at the height of anger or emotionally distraught. When you are under unusual stress from work, family issues, or other circumstances, be more conscious of your words and actions as you respond to challenges from and with your children. Don't use objects to administer discipline that could inflict personal injury on your child.

"Fathers, do not provoke your children to anger, but bring them up in the discipline and instruction of the Lord" (Ephesians 6:4).

Don't allow life circumstances, internal pressures, or your child's negative behavior to result in your engaging in abusive behavior toward your child.

15

PRESCRIPTION FOR BROKENNESS

When Your Child Strays

Thomas' father is more passionate about only one other thing than the church he pastors—his family. Because I have known him for more than ten years, his commitment to being a godly father is unquestioned in my mind. *He loves God and has served his family well.* Yet his son has still chosen to rebel against him and God.

His son strayed away from the truth he regularly heard and the pattern of life modeled for him throughout his childhood. He is now paying the penalty for his rebellion by being confined for a period of time, against his will, by law enforcement officials. His father's words to me could easily describe the feelings of many parents: "I didn't get a good return on my investment."

THE PAIN OF DISAPPOINTMENT

What happens when your child disappoints you? Your heart hurts. It feels like someone took a knife and a cut a hole in the middle of your chest—and now there is a slow leak you don't know how to stop. That's how it feels when one of your children deeply disappoints you. Very few experiences in life hurt quite so bad.

I know. I have been there too.

At first, your mind wanders down a lot of dead-end streets. *How could they do that to me?* The feeling that you have been betrayed temporarily stuns you. Then, if you are like most parents, you begin the long journey down the road of self-induced guilt, reviewing all your personal failures. *If only I had . . . I should have . . . I wish that we had done that differently.*

If you are not careful, those roaming thoughts will cause you to sink into a mental and emotional quicksand that will paralyze you.

BE REAL

I remember a sobering conversation when Annie and I were discussing a situation where one of our children had violated our trust. As we began to talk, we went down the road of self-condemnation and slipped into the quicksand of a sense of parental failure. I was sinking fast.

Then the quiet, wise counsel of my gentle wife helped me gain my bearings. "But Larry, what about when you were growing up? Did you ever disappoint your parents?"

Enough said.

My mind reviewed my childhood and adult failures. Those words carried me back to the simple truth—we *all* have our share of personal failures. Then the words of Scripture reminded me of my personal shortcomings and the humanity of my children:

> If we say that we have no sin, we are deceiving ourselves and the truth is not in us. If we confess our sins, He is faithful and righteous to forgive us our sins and to cleanse us from all unrighteousness. If we say that we have not sinned, we make Him a liar and His Word is not in us. (1 John 1:8–10)

The Bible reminds me that we all fail, but it also makes clear that our failure does not have to be fatal. Neither does the failure of our children.

Very few children go through life without some physical scrapes and bruises from personal falls. The same is true for their mental and emotional lives. "To err is human." Expect it.

BE MATURE

The question is not really whether our children will experience some level of failure in their lifetimes. Our children will fail to meet our expectations. The question is how we as parents handle it when they fail to live up to our expectations.

When you are tempted to get lost traveling down the road of self-condemnation, and the phrase *If only I had . . .* dominates your thoughts, and you are going down a lot of mental dead-end streets, stop and think carefully. Make a conscious, mature decision to get off that road. Sober reflection on Scripture will help you arrive at a balanced biblical perspective.

REMEMBER THAT CHILDHOOD FAILURE DOESN'T ALWAYS EQUAL PARENTAL SHORTCOMINGS

Remember Adam and Eve? They had a perfect environment, all their needs were met, and they had complete access to their Father. They still chose to disobey.

We learn a simple lesson from the first chapters of the Bible—disobedience on the part of the follower does not always indicate failure in the life of the leader. The application of that principle to parenting is clear. Shortcomings in the life of a child do not necessarily mean that his parents failed to provide the guidance and support the child needed to make right choices.

GO TO THE SCRIPTURES

Yet even if you know you did your best, *that does not stop the pain.* It still hurts when your child strays away from God and your teaching. What do you do when the pain from a straying child is present in your life?

Friends and counselors are available on whom you may call. That may be a wise option. But the very first option should be the counsel of God's Word. "Your word is a lamp to my feet and a light to my path" (Psalm 119:105).

MIMIC THE PATTERN OF GOD

Sometimes we forget that the Bible not only gives us a wonderful picture of the glory of God but also clearly shows us the brokenness of man. There are many illustrations of human failure in the Bible, but very few rival the story of the Prodigal Son in Luke 15:11–32 as a place for us to glean some insights to help us deal with the times of struggle in the lives of our children. We can learn powerful lessons from Luke 15.

The experience of the Prodigal gives us a wonderful snapshot of how to respond to our children when they stray away from God's standards and our values. It gives us a picture of how a father responds to a drifting child and a glimpse into the heart of God. The Prodigal Son's father never stopped hoping that his son would return, and when the young man *did* return, he ran to greet him. A great celebration was held. God carefully places the story of the Prodigal Son among other illustrations describing brokenness so that we can learn about the heart of God.

> Now all the tax collectors and the sinners were coming near Him to listen to Him. Both the Pharisees and the Scribes began to grumble saying, "This man receives sinners and eats with them."
>
> So He told them a parable saying, "What man among you, if he has a hundred sheep and has lost one of them, does not leave the ninety-nine in the open pasture and go after the one which is lost until he finds it? When he has found it, he lays it on his shoulders, rejoicing. And when he comes home, he calls together his friends and his neighbors, saying to them, 'Rejoice with me, for I have found my sheep which was lost!' I tell you that in the same way, there will be more joy in heaven over one sinner who repents than over ninety-nine righteous persons who need no repentance.
>
> "Or what woman, if she has ten silver coins and loses one coin, does not light a lamp and sweep the house and search carefully until she finds it? When she has found it, she calls together her friends and neighbors, saying, 'Rejoice with me, for I have found the coin which I had lost!' In the same way, I tell you, there is joy in the presence of the angels of God over one sinner who repents." (Luke 15:1–10)

These parables powerfully demonstrate how God feels about a believer who strays.

1. God goes after a straying believer with intensity.
2. God celebrates repentance by a lost believer.

God never gives up on a straying believer. The parables of the Lost Sheep, the Lost Coin, and the Prodigal Son provide a wonderful backdrop to illustrate how important each one of His children is to God. He never gives up on His children.

You and I are witnesses to that truth. What would have happened to you if God had given up on you during one of the periods of rebellion in your life? Thank God neither of us knows the answer to that question. I don't think the answer would be pretty. His love for us compels Him to keep hoping and praying that when we stray we will eventually return to Him.

LET YOUR CHILD ENROLL IN THE "UNIVERSITY OF EXPERIENCE"

God knows that sometimes our return has to follow some hard lessons from life. In the same way, God teaches that straying children have to learn from their life experiences.

We have all heard the phrase "What goes up must come down." It is a simple way of describing the law of gravity. The law of gravity is a natural law that affects all physical objects. Simply stated, every physical object that is thrown into the air will eventually come down.

In the same way that the law of gravity relates to physical objects, so it is sometimes that the disappointment that comes from personal failures will cause a child to see the error of his ways and turn back to God and the expectations of his parents.

There is the temptation to see fame and personal ability as passes to the easy life. The words "You don't know who I am" can be the cry of a talented youth whose heart has been hardened by a lifetime of exemptions from the consequences of his personal actions. He hasn't learned that eventually he will have to pay a price for misdeeds. Athletic ability or business talent should not extend him unearned exemption from the results of a short-circuited ability to distinguish right from wrong. While your children are still young enough to receive training at home, allow them to learn from the "University of Experience" that you supervise.

DON'T CHANGE THE GRADES

A well-known pastor, Dr. E. K. Bailey, described the power of experience to change our behavior this way: "Sometimes people don't change until the pain of remaining the same becomes too great." Another way of saying it: "Sometimes it is only when we experience the consequences of our poor choices that we have a reason to change." In Galatians 6, the Scripture clearly communicates that God holds every believer accountable for his personal actions. "Do not be deceived, God is not mocked; for whatever a man sows, this he will also reap" (Galatians 6:7).

Your precious child is no exception. The principle found in Galatians 6:7 applies to him. He needs to learn academics as he goes through childhood, but very few lessons will make as much impact as the lessons that come from experiencing the consequences of poor personal choices. I have seen many well-meaning parents who have hampered the growth of their children by protecting them from the consequences of their personal choices in an unhealthy way.

DON'T GIVE YOUR CHILD THE PAIN OF THE EASY ROAD

Sandra's story found a place in my mind more than seventeen years ago that I still reflect on today. She was seventeen years old and ready to return home after spending almost a year living in a facility for children considered delinquent. As she approached the end of her time under court-ordered placement at the facility, she experienced a challenging emotional contradiction.

She had made tremendous progress during her year at the facility, yet her sadness caused shadows of depression to cross her face. As I sat down and asked her why she was sad, her words etched a place in my mind. She said eleven sober words about her parents. "They didn't love me enough to stop me from hurting myself."

She then described parents who, no doubt, loved their daughter but didn't know how to confront her. When she rebelled, they took what she thought was the "easy road" of nonconfrontation. Apparently they thought that giving their daughter severe consequences for her misbehavior would alienate her. Instead, alienation came from a lack of consequences.

Looking back, she interpreted the lack of confrontation by her parents as a diminished expression of their love. I will never forget that conversation. I will forever remember the "pain of the easy road."

SHOW YOUR SUPPORT

Wait a minute! That does not mean that you give him the impression you have written him off. In spite of his failure, let him know you will never give up on him. Even though your frustration may make you want to quit. You shouldn't. You can't.

Remember, that child was given to you as a gift from God. He needs your support more now than he ever has before.

REMEMBER THE GRACE OF GOD TOWARD YOU

God didn't give up on you or me. He hasn't rendered out to me in a mean-spirited way all the consequences that might have come for my actions. No! God always deals with me in a redemptive manner.

He is always concerned about my needs as well as His standard of holiness. As you think about your child's failure, reflect on God's grace toward you when you fail. Strive to extend the same kind of grace to your children that God has given to you.

I learned that lesson by observation recently through a conversation with a dear Christian friend. A well-known Christian leader's son decided he would adopt a sexual lifestyle that ran in direct opposition to the teaching and model of his parents. The parents have made it clear they don't approve of their son's sexual behavior, but somehow they have communicated a deep love for his person even in the midst of his sin.

I remember well the lines of anguish on the face of that young man's mother as she described their pain. But I remember more the depth of love and forgiveness the father and mother extended to their son as they continually showed him the grace of God through their actions. I quietly voiced a prayer that day that I hope to never forget: "Lord, help me to show the same kind of grace to my children when they fail."

BE PATIENT: KEEP THE WINDOW OF YOUR HEART OPEN

The picture in the story of the Prodigal gives us a powerful example to imitate. The words of the Scripture say, "But while he was still *a long way off,* his father saw him and felt compassion for him" (italics added). The father in the story of the Prodigal gives us a picture of God's disposition toward us. God's heart is always open for us to return to Him.

Don't let your heart get cold. Bitterness can form a callus over your heart if you are not careful. Your child's misbehavior or rebellion is not outside the reach of God's grasp. Too many parents have been overcome by a pattern of failure in a child's life and have simply given up. Your child *can* change.

It is important that you show your child that you still see his potential even when he is distant from you in his behavior. He needs to know that you believe he can change. The young man in the story of the Prodigal knew he could always come back home. Your child needs to know he can come back home when he is ready to repent.

KEEP THE LIGHTS ON

Keep the lights on by learning to focus on your child's potential rather than dwelling on his problems. Focusing on your child's potential will diminish his feelings of personal rejection when you correct his misbehavior. You could very easily continually remind him of his failure to live up to your standards. If you only focus on his problems, he will lose his sense of value and significance to you and to God.

Don't compromise. Keep the truth ever before your child. But the message will not be complete if it does not contain a spirit of redemption: *"Our hearts are broken but we still love you. When God opens your eyes to see the pain you have caused us, we will be waiting for you. We long for the day to embrace you with a sense that you are free from the bondage that grips your life. When you are ready, there is a place for you in our home."*

Don't stop sending encouraging messages. *"You can overcome this and we will help you . . . Don't give up on yourself . . . Keep trying . . . Life will be so much better for you when you overcome this . . . "* can all be powerful expressions of parental confidence and keep hope alive in the heart of your child. By the way, you *have* to do that—keep hope alive in his heart.

AFTER THEY REPENT, GIVE THEM A FRESH NEW START

Parental focus on past failures can weigh a child down so much he can't move into the future. Too many parents hold their children hostage to past mistakes. "Remember, when you failed . . . This is just like the time before . . . I knew this would happen again . . ." This can stifle your child's motivation. Creating a chain of negative memories can tie your child down to a perpetual feeling of failure.

Celebrate your child's future rather than keeping him chained to the past. After your child has admitted his failure and changed direction, give him a fresh start. The father in Luke 15 is a good model to follow.

> "But the father said to his slaves, 'Quickly bring out the best robe and put it on him, and put a ring on his hand and sandals on his feet; and bring the fattened calf, kill it, and let us eat and celebrate; for this son of mine was dead and has come to life again; he was lost and has been found.' And they began to celebrate." (Luke 15:22–24)

Let everyone who knows about your child's past mistakes know also that he is committed to a positive future. An unknown author described his feelings in a way that is instructive for each one of us as parents. The author gives the picture of the heart of a person who desperately needs help but doesn't know how to ask for it. This person's story could be your child's when he feels overwhelmed.

PLEASE HEAR WHAT I'M NOT SAYING

Don't be fooled by me. Don't be fooled by the face I wear. For I wear a thousand masks that I'm afraid to take off, and none of them are me. Pretending is an art that's second nature with me, but don't be fooled, for God's sake. I give the impression that I'm secure, that all is sunny and unruffled with me, within as well as without that confidence is my name and coolness my game;

that the waters are calm and I'm in command, and that I need no one. But don't believe me . . . Please.

My surface may seem smooth, but my surface is my mask. Beneath it lies no complacence. Beneath dwells the real me—in confusion, in fear, in aloneness. But I hide this. I don't want anybody to know it. I panic at the thought of my weakness and fear being exposed. That's why I frantically create a mask to hide behind, a nonchalant, sophisticated façade to help me pretend; to shield me from the glance that knows. But such a glance is precisely my salvation—my *only* salvation. And I know it. That is, if it's followed by love. It's the only thing that will assure me of what I can't assure myself, that I am worth something.

But I don't tell you this—I don't dare. I'm afraid to. I'm afraid you'll think less of me, that you'll laugh at me—and your laugh would kill me. I'm afraid that deep down, I'm nothing, that I'm no good, and that you'll see this and reject me. So I play my game, my desperate game, with a façade of assurance without, and a trembling child within . . .

I fight against the very thing I cry out for. But I am told that love is stronger than walls, and in this lies my hope. Please try to beat down those walls with firm hands, but with gentle hands for a child is very sensitive . . .

FAITH STEPS

1. If your child strays from your teaching, identify areas you need to change and make the adjustments.

2. After you have made any personal adjustments God leads you to make, resist the tendency to fall into an emotional bondage to false guilt if your child fails.

3. Expect your child to show his imperfections from time to time.

4. Focus on an attitude of expectancy that your child will repent and come home when he strays.

5. Be redemptive. Resist the temptation to hold your child hostage to past failures after he has confessed and repented.

A PARENT'S PRAYER

Dear Lord, Thank You for the opportunity to love my child, even when he fails. Help me to see my child with Your eyes. Keep my heart from hardening in the face of repeated expressions of misbehavior. Give me a spirit of restoration and not condemnation. Protect us from the pain of the easy road. Allow me to remember my own imperfections as I see the frailties of my child's life. My deep desire is to allow my child to experience Your grace through me. Amen.

PARENTING INSIGHTS

SPECIAL CARE INSTRUCTIONS

Research Highlight: Your Child and Sexuality

Recent research highlights some important facts about childhood sexuality that will help give you the background you need to equip your child to express his sexuality in a way that honors God.[1]

RESEARCH HIGHLIGHTS

- According to a recent survey, 66 percent of females and 67.1 percent of males are sexually active by the time they reach their senior year of high school.
- Teens are diagnosed with 3 million new cases of sexually transmitted diseases every year.
- Forty-three percent of all teenagers who get pregnant have an abortion.
- HIV has risen to be the seventh leading cause of death among females between the ages of fifteen to twenty-four.
- In excess of 500,000 teenagers have babies in the United States each year. One fifth of the annual births in this country are attributed to teen mothers. The fastest growing category of parents are in the ten- to fourteen-year-old age range.

Christianity Today cited survey results indicating that, although parents were considered by teens their most trustworthy source of information about their sexuality, sources such as peers, sex-education classes, television, and magazines far outranked parents as the place most teens actually got their sex education.

RESEARCH APPLICATIONS

1. Model moral purity for your child.
2. Learn how to communicate with your child about sex in a clear and plain manner.
3. Educate your child about the physical and emotional dimensions of his sexuality.
4. Equip your child with the emotional strength to resist allowing sex to meet his emotional needs.
5. Encourage your child to make a commitment to sexual abstinence until marriage.
6. Teach your child to set boundaries in his interpersonal relationships.
7. Help your child recognize the signals he will hear and feel when he is in the "danger zone."

"Or do you not know that your body is a temple of the Holy Spirit who is in you, whom you have from God, and that you are not your own? For you have been bought with a price; therefore glorify God in your body" (1 Corinthians 6:19–20).

Prepare your child for responsible sexuality by modeling, instructing, and giving him regular guidance as he moves from childhood to adulthood. Commit yourself to becoming your child's primary sex-education instructor according to the Scripture.

16

NO RETURNS ACCEPTED

Handling the Struggle of Caring for Your Child

Rosanne lightened my spirit after a busy week of ministry. She had a level of energy and enthusiasm that was contagious. Her love for Christ was refreshing.

Our first few moments sitting beside each other on American Flight 2239 was what I usually experienced on other plane flights. As she let me move to my window seat, we greeted each other cordially. Then she pulled out a book, and I leaned back in my seat to catch a few minutes of overdue rest.

After about forty-five minutes into the trip, I pulled out the papers that had to be graded for my graduate school leadership class and started to read. Her voice soon broke my concentration with a very simple question I knew would be followed by others. I confess my knowledge that the grades for the semester had to be turned in over the next couple of days initially kept my concentration on the papers. She said, "Is Dallas your final stop?" I barely looked up and replied, "Yes. My family and home are in Dallas."

A DIVINE APPOINTMENT

About fifteen minutes later another question came. "What do you do?" I looked up to make eye contact. "I work for a group of ministries in Chicago called the Moody Bible Institute." Her eyes lit up as a big smile came across her face. Then it was clear to me I was in for a long conversation.

"My grandfather went to Moody a bunch of years ago." I also found she was a fifth grade teacher in Chicago and often shared what she learned from Moody radio with her students. She told them about what God was teaching her on the "Jesus station," referring to Moody radio. Her excitement was irresistible. I put aside my papers and we launched into a conversation that lasted for the duration of the flight from Chicago to Dallas.

From time to time she would say, "I am keeping you from your work." Then I said, "Don't worry about my work. God will take care of that." Strangely, our roles had reversed. I became the questioner and she the responder. It was soon clear to me that God wanted me to learn a few things from Rosanne. She had a lot to teach me. During the next hour and a half I learned a lot about Rosanne and gleaned some life lessons I will never forget.

PROTECTED BY GOD'S SACRED DESK

Rosanne had given birth to three children. One of her children was born with serious physical and emotional challenges that greatly impacted the family. This child is now an adult living alone, but Rosanne still devotes a lot of her time to making sure all his needs are met. She told me that this particular child had been in the hospital more than two hundred times over the first twenty-six years of his life since she started counting.

Yet Rosanne exuded an excitement about her relationship with God that was obviously something special. Her faith had an authenticity that intrigued and challenged me. Her response to the problems in her life was an incredible example to me of the perspective a parent should have when she faces difficult circumstances with her child.

The problems for Rosanne's child were physical and emotional. Your child's challenge may not be either of these; it may be behavioral or academic. Your child could demonstrate behavior that goes against the grain of everything you model and teach.

That's possible, you know. Your child is a free moral agent. That simply means that your child has the capacity to make her own decisions. Here is the real challenge—*her decisions may not match your expectations.* What are you going to do then?

That is where biblical parenting is important. Biblical parenting does not guarantee the absence of problems. Any idea that you as a parent can guarantee the total absence of problems in your child's life (physical, emotional, social, and spiritual) is not rooted in Scripture. Biblical parenting calls for a godly response from you as a parent when the problems come.

One of the questions I asked Rosanne was, "What has God taught you through your parenting experience with your child who has special needs?"

Her answer was priceless. She said, "I have the learned the truth of the phrase 'Nothing happens in the life of the believer without going across God's sacred desk.' God has a purpose for everything. . . . I am a better person than I was before. . . . I learned that I am not better than anyone else. . . . Our whole family looks at life differently."

May I remind you that if you know Christ there is nothing that can come into your life without its "passing across God's sacred desk." There will be times during your parenting when you will experience pain. Your initial and sometimes sustained response will be to wonder whether God knows about your pain. He does—and He cares about it.

That is where the truth of Romans 8:28 is a balm of comfort and consolation. "And we know that God causes all things to work together for good to those who love God, to those who are called according to His purpose." That verse tells us that God converts every experience for those who love Him into a positive benefit, even the negative ones.

MAKING YOU LIKE CHRIST

It also serves to remind us that God uses everything—including your experiences as a parent—to conform you to the image of Christ. Remember, while you are building into the life of your child, God wants to build into *your* life as *His* child. You are in process too.

God will use the joys and challenges of the parenting process to make you more like Jesus Christ. Expect challenges. When you experience a difficult parenting moment, stop and ask yourself the question, *What is God trying to teach me?* God wants to make you more like Christ.

Don't be so overwhelmed with the pain and challenge of parenting that you forget that God has a process at work in your life too. We often tell our children that when difficult times come, trust God. We sometimes forget that the parenting process gives us an opportunity to practice what we preach. That is not easy.

I remember one of my professors at Dallas Seminary, Howard Hendricks, who has logged many miles as a parent and as an influence on Christian leaders, saying once of dealing with hard times that "everybody wants the product, but nobody wants the process." All of us, as Christian parents, want to be like Christ. A key quality will be not allowing childhood disobedience to slow us down or distract us from parenting challenges.

MAKE PERSONAL ADJUSTMENTS

Don't assume the trouble is only your child's fault. Sometimes our personal failures can short-circuit our child's success. Notice what Exodus says:

> "You shall not worship [idols] or serve them; for I, the Lord your God, am a jealous God, visiting the iniquity of the fathers on the children, on the third and the fourth generations of those who hate Me, but show lovingkindness to thousands, to those who love Me and keep My commandments." (Exodus 20:5–6)

Ask yourself some basic questions. *Do I have some habits that may be influencing my child? Are some tendencies in my life being expressed as full-blown traits in my child's life? Do I need to change my personal routine so that my child will be more carefully served? Is there a sin I need to confess and repent?*

If you recognize changes you need to make, do it. Make the adjustments in your life as a parent so that you and your child can experience the growth God wants you to have. Be willing to acknowledge your part of a problem that may exist in your child's life.

DEAL WITH SPIRITUAL STRONGHOLDS

In fact, if your child experiences repeated failures in the same area, a period of fasting may be in order. Sometimes Satan sets up a stronghold in your child's life. That can only be overcome by looking for a solution through an intervention by the supernatural power of God. This kind of struggle reminds us of the truth found in Ephesians 6:12: "For our struggle is not against flesh and blood, but against the rulers, against the powers, against the world forces of this darkness, against the spiritual forces of wickedness in the heavenly places."

Sometimes you simply don't have the power to deal with the spiritual forces at work. Of course, you need God's power for every challenge, but some challenges require a more intense focus. It seems there is something happening you do not understand and cannot explain. Prayer and fasting may be the only way to reach a solution.

LET GOD HAVE HIS WAY

When we see our children struggle, it is hard to relinquish them into God's hand. Yet we must all arrive at the point where we say, "Have your way, Lord, in my child's life and in my life as a parent."

During my time of interaction with Rosanne on the plane, she told me about how she arrived at the point of acknowledging that her child's life belonged to God. That came after many times of screaming out as she followed the ambulance carrying her son to the hospital, "God, You can't have him! He is mine." Finally, during one of those more than two hundred trips, Rosanne said, "Lord, he's yours."

That did not stop the struggle in the life of Rosanne's child, but it did cause a truce in the war of soul she was having with God. For Rosanne, it was a key moment in her personal journey toward emotional peace. As you face challenges in your role as a parent, the war of soul with God can cease by your simply saying, "God, my child belongs to You; have Your way."

If you have not already said that, perhaps that acknowledgment can be a key moment in your journey toward personal peace as a parent.

DO ALL YOU CAN

What does God want you to do when difficult times come as you seek to guide your children?

Do all you can.

I believe there is a "Parenting Reflex" you can practice that is based on Scripture. It will produce a confidence in your heart that you have done all that God expects you to do. This Parenting Reflex has five steps.

Read—what the Bible says about the area of concern.
Pray—to God for insight and direction.
Reflect—on the testimony and counsel of others (advice, books, other instruction).
Listen—to the guidance of the Holy Spirit.
Obey—what Christ leads you to do.

God wants you to do all you can to remedy the situation. He wants you to seek advice and counsel. For example, you can make sure your child understands how God views her behavior.

WHEN YOU HAVE DONE ALL YOU CAN, JUST STAND

"Having done everything, . . . stand firm" (Ephesians 6:13). When spiritual pressures come, the apostle Paul says, we need to put on the full armor of God and stand firm in Him. That is solemn advice for every serious believer for dealing with the challenges that come his way and solemn advice for us as parents. We may go through painful situations with our children. Our children may break our hearts. Sometimes, when we have given our all in the parenting pressures, failure has still come. Those are times we need to remember that when we have done everything we know to do the moment comes to just stand and rest in God. He has a purpose and a plan and will bring us through the storm.

FAITH STEPS

1. Expect challenges and remember that biblical parenting does not guarantee the absence of problems.

2. When you face challenges as a parent, look for ways that God can develop your character through the process.

3. Show willingness to acknowledge and correct your problems as a parent.
4. When you face problems, always practice the "Parenting Reflex."

   Read what the Bible says about your area of concern.
   Pray and ask God for insight and direction.

Reflect on the counsel of others
Listen to the guidance of the Holy Spirit
Obey what Christ leads you to do.

5. Don't quit in the face of challenges; instead, stand with as strong a support system as possible.

A PARENT'S PRAYER

Lord, Help me to recognize that nothing can come into my life without its first passing Your "sacred desk." Thank You for using all my parenting experiences to make me more like Christ in my attitude and actions. Lord, help me make personal adjustments when my life is contributing to failure in my child's life. Lord, free my child from spiritual strongholds that keep her spirit captive. I want You to have Your way in my life and the life of my child. My desire is to respond to challenges in a way that pleases You. Lord, when I have done all I can, help me to stand. Amen.

PARENTING INSIGHTS

SPECIAL CARE INSTRUCTIONS

Research Highlight: Your Child's Special Needs

All children do not share the same physical, emotional, and intellectual characteristics, but all children do share the same access to God's love and concern. Your child is special to God, and the special needs and challenges she may have should be addressed to the best of your ability. In order to do that it may be helpful to understand the broad range of special needs affecting children. The Individuals with Disabilities Education Act (IDEA) defines "children with disabilities" as having any of the following types of disabilities: autism, deafness, deafness-blindness, hearing impairments (including deafness), mental retardation, multiple disabilities, orthopedic impairments, other health impairments, serious emotional disturbance, specific learning disabilities, speech or language impairments, traumatic brain injury, and visual impairments (including blindness). The Individuals with Disabilities Education Act guarantees that every child will receive a free public education that is able to meet her individual needs.[1]

RESEARCH HIGHLIGHTS

- One out of ten children in the U.S. is estimated to be classified as an exceptional child, with a total of 8 million children in this category.
- Approximately 2–3 percent of the population below the age of nineteen years old is mentally retarded.
- Estimates conclude that at least 4 percent of all school-age children are learning disabled.
- About 5 million children have been diagnosed with asthma, and it is the most common chronic illness among children.
- According to the National Information Center for Children and Youth with Disabilities, "The Education of the Handicapped Act, Public Law (P.L.) 94–142, was passed by Congress in 1975 and amended by P.L. 99– 457 in 1986 to ensure that all children with

disabilities would have a free, appropriate public education available to them which would meet their unique needs. It was again amended in 1990 and the name was changed to IDEA."

RESEARCH APPLICATIONS

1. Treat your child and any child you encounter with complete dignity in spite of the disabilities or personal challenges that child may have.
2. Teach your child that God views her as a person with great worth and dignity.
3. Make sure your child's needs are properly assessed and diagnosed.
4. Learn about the programs, services, and resources available to help address your child's needs.
5. Aggressively access the programs, services, and resources available to your child.
6. Develop supportive relationships with other parents or groups who understand and can assist you through your journey.
7. If necessary, seek ministerial or professional counseling and support to assist you in taking care of yourself and your child.

"As He passed by, He saw a man blind from birth. And His disciples asked Him, "Rabbi, who sinned, this man or his parents, that he would be born blind?" Jesus answered, "It was neither that this man sinned, nor his parents; but it was so that the works of God might be displayed in him" (John 9:1–3).

God is concerned that every child, including those with special needs, achieves His full purpose for that child's life. Use every resource available to you to help your children. Their lives may be radically different because you did your best.

17

DEALING WITH EMERGENCIES

Addressing Serious Behavior Problems

I had a number of significant experiences during my tenure as superintendent of a juvenile institution. One of those involved a young man named Harry. Harry was approximately sixteen years old. He had not had an easy stay at the facility, but finally turned things around and was about ready to be discharged to return home.

Literally days before Harry was scheduled to be discharged he was involved in a serious physical conflict with one of his peers. His actions confused all the staff. Why would Harry, just days away from being discharged, get pulled into a conflict that would cancel his release or at the very least put it off by months?

ALL BEHAVIOR MAKES A STATEMENT ABOUT WHAT'S GOING ON INSIDE

I asked Harry, "Why did you get involved in that fight when you knew it would cause you to have to stay here a lot longer?" I was very surprised but enlightened by his response. "Sir, I am not ready to be released. I don't think I can handle it." He was afraid of going back into a world of what he perceived as past failures and broken relationships. So Harry sabotaged his own success at the institution to prevent what he feared as an even greater failure in the world.

His honesty illustrated a simple point. He had a need for security that caused him to violate the security of others. Was his behavior justified? No! Did he have a legitimate need? Yes!

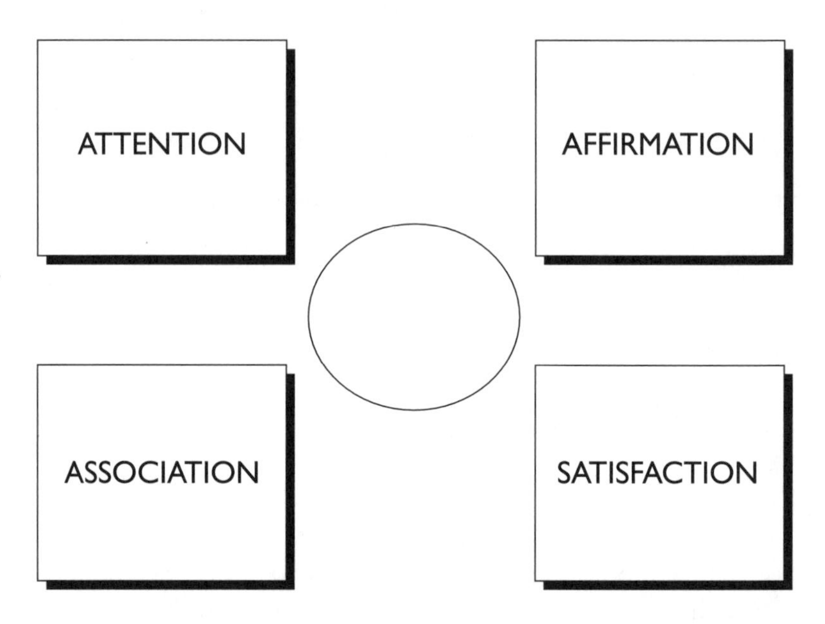

All behavior is directed toward gaining attention, affirmation, association, and/or some type of satisfaction. Just like Harry, your child's individual actions are expressed with a goal in view. Sometimes the goal is conscious, but in many cases an unmet need your child isn't fully "conscious of" is driving his behavior.

You have to make the commitment to not simply look at your child's behavior from the viewpoint of how it affects you, but see it from the viewpoint of what it says about the needs of your child. You also have to try to put yourself in the place of your child and try to examine his actions with empathy and understanding.

The Bible gives us a model of how to respond to problems in the lives of others that should certainly include our children. "We urge you, brethren, admonish the unruly, encourage the fainthearted, help the weak, be patient with everyone" (1 Thessalonians 5:14).

The Bible gives us a clear challenge. When a person is going through a personal challenge, our response should always be characterized by empathy and patience.

Our children deserve the kind of empathy and patience God expects us to express to other people in general. Personal challenges in the life of our children are invitations for us to show empathy and patience toward them and respond to their sometimes unarticulated cries for help.

PLEASE MEET MY NEED

When your child displays very negative behavior there is a very important process you must go through. You must take the time to try to understand what your child is feeling and thinking. It takes a little longer to do that, but when your child displays a pattern of problem behavior, you must do it. Ask yourself the question, *What need is my child seeking to have met?*

A study by Prison Fellowship Ministries demonstrated that all young people, even "delinquent" youth, have a need for trust, power, purpose, mastery, and self-sacrifice.[1] Your child's problem behavior is focused on meeting his need for some level of satisfaction, stimulation, affirmation, attention, or recognition.

Be careful that you don't get so overwhelmed by your child's behavior he gets lost in the process. How do you respond to the behavior of your child when sometimes his actions are so complex? Don't be overwhelmed with the potential response to that question.

Start with the basics, like the child's diet

Sometimes your child's misbehavior is simply the result of a need being unmet. Studies have shown how critical it is to make sure basic needs, such as a changed diet, are not driving childhood misbehavior. Francisco Contreras reports:

> We all need good food to maintain optimum health. When we eat right, we are healthier—in our bodies and our minds. One recent study demonstrated that well.

The administration of public schools in New York, together with state government, removed all foods offered at the school cafeteria that had artificial color and flavor additives, as well as other types of additives and preservatives. They also significantly reduced products with sugar and refined flour.

The study concluded that the one million students in New York's 803 public schools raised their grades an average of 39 to 54.9 percent during the length of the study. Not a single change was made in the curriculum. These impressive statistics were a direct result of the changes in the diet during school hours. The scientists concluded that if changes had been extended to the diet at the home, the results would have been extraordinary.

Another series of studies made of youth detention centers involved 8,076 youngsters from 12 correctional centers.

Chemical additives, sugar and refined flour were withdrawn from their diets. At the end of these studies, the aggressive and destructive behaviors of the detained youngsters diminished 47 percent.

In Virginia, 275 young detained delinquents with a criminal background were given a healthy diet for two years. During that period jail theft declined 77 percent, insubordination 55 percent, and hyperactivity 65 percent.

Another study in Los Angeles involved 1,382 teenage offenders. Again, the results were positive. There was a reduction of 44 percent in their delinquent behavior and suicide attempts.

The above studies demonstrate that when youngsters (and adults) follow a healthy diet—including highly nutritious foods such as vegetables, fruits, and cereals, and excluding refined sugars, artificial colors, flavor additives and chemical preservatives—both physical and mental health improve.[2]

Try your best to avoid underestimating the significance of things as simple as water and diet. Start with the most basic areas of need to make sure that these are not the problem areas. Your child may simply need you to change his diet and/or add some much-needed nutritional support.

Look for the presence of a biblical sense of hope

Beyond the physical needs being met in times of crisis, it is important to make sure your child's need is not a need for a sense of security. Sometimes your child may do something that is in your mind unbelievable. The behavior may be a sign that they have lost a sense of hope.

The Bible makes clear that a loss of hope can be debilitating in a person's life. The image powerfully conveyed in the book of Proverbs illustrates what can happen in the life of a child. "Hope deferred makes the heart sick, but desire fulfilled is a tree of life" (Proverbs 13:12).

Your child needs a sense of hope. That raises a natural question: What is hope? The most basic definition of hope is "to cherish a desire with the expectation of fulfillment."

Hope takes on several practical forms for a child in distress and facing a difficult situation.

- **Hope** can be a deep desire for the pain of loneliness to stop.
- **Hope** can be a craving for affirmation from a meaningful individual in the child's life.
- **Hope** can be the anticipation that dreams that have been nursed will become reality.
- **Hope** is wrapped up in efforts to not be rejected when personal weaknesses are exposed.
- **Hope** is the yearning for the cycle of failure in life to be broken by the satisfaction of some kind of victory.
- **Hope** is the expectation that his tomorrow can be something better than what he experienced yesterday.
- **Hope** is the sense that his need to simply be noticed will be fulfilled.

What happens when hope is deferred in the life of a child? Many things can take place.

- Loss of hope can cause a child to abandon his family.
- Lack of hope can cause a child to drop out of school.
- Lack of hope can cause a child to self-medicate himself with drugs.
- Lack of hope can cause a child to run away from home.
- Loss of hope can cause a child to take his own life.
- Lack of hope can cause a child to rob someone rather than work.
- Lack of hope can cause a child to bond with destructive, manipulative people.

Sometimes the internal struggle in the heart of a child breaks out into strange behavior. How do you know when a child is in emotional turmoil?

There are some clear warning signs that indicate your child's emotional balance is in jeopardy. Be on the alert for the following warning signs that will give you a window into the fact your child needs special personal and emotional support.

WARNING SIGNS OF CURRENT OR IMPENDING CRISIS

- Expressing feelings of rejection
- Depression
- Consistent display of uncontrollable anger
- Cruelty to animals
- Fascination with guns and other weapons
- Isolation from normal peer group
- Exclusive association with antisocial friends
- Dramatic mood swings
- Persistent problem with performing school assignments
- Wearing gang-related clothing and other symbols
- Obsession with violence and conflict
- Shift in personal care habits
- Exhibiting aggressive behavior
- Intense rebellion against established authorities

One of these signs alone may not be an indication of serious problems. But if you see a combination of these warning signs, it may indicate that you need to seek special support.[3]

The power of a peer support network

"Please notice me!" That is the heart cry of every child. Your child is no exception. Sometimes your child's need for attention is so great he makes decisions that are detrimental to other people or self-destructive.

The need for peer attention and support can be powerful in the life of a child. A recent *USA Today* feature illustrated the limits a child will go to for attention as it told about the experience of a young thirteen-year-old boy mimicking a scene from an MTV prank show.

The young boy was hospitalized and placed on a critical condition status after he set himself on fire. He and a fourteen-year-old friend were arrested and charged with reckless endangerment. They were trying to recreate a scene from an MTV episode that featured Johnny Knoxville as a human barbecue. This tragic episode illustrated how vulnerable the boys were to the ideas promoted in that television episode.

It also demonstrated how the boys' need for attention temporarily cost them their freedom and put their lives and health at risk. That is why the Scripture gives such a clear warning to avoid people who have values that distract from spiritual growth and maturity. "Do not be deceived: 'Bad company corrupts good morals'" (1 Corinthians 15:33).

Teach your child how to meet his needs in correct ways

It is OK for your child to have a need for satisfaction, stimulation, affirmation, attention, or recognition. The problem is not the presence of the need. It is how your child meets those needs. That is why it is important for you to teach your child how to meet his needs in an appropriate way.

If your child feels that no one is there to support him or hold him accountable, there is the potential that he will make some very poor decisions. The reason and method the child uses to meet his needs determines whether his thoughts and actions fall in the categories of good or bad. If you practice biblical parenting, you can seek to train your child to use righteous methods to meet his needs for satisfaction, stimulation, affirmation, attention, and recognition.

Intervention from a biblical framework in times of crisis structures the child's life experiences to encourage and reward behavior that is consistent with the teachings of Scripture, while at the same time it discourages behavior that dishonors God and uses appropriate consequences for that behavior. It is a proactive, positive, constructive process that always has the best interests of the child in mind.

Biblical intervention requires several levels of parental activity. Since discipline and intervention from a biblical framework is essentially teaching, it begins with the model of your life as the first phase of the process. Your life should illustrate the behavior you desire to see in the life of the child.

Sometimes your child may not recognize what you are doing or may not understand it as in his best interest. That is why it is critical that, in addition to modeling desired behavior, you give your child practical instruction on how each behavior should work out in his life. You owe it to your child to make sure he understands your expectations of him.

Your child will sometimes fail to live up to your parental expectations. It is critical for you as the parent to determine whether your child's failure is a reflection of rebellion or simply expresses his personal weakness. Weakness and failure should be treated in a different way from childhood rebellion. Failure should motivate you to instruct and correct your child. Sometimes failure indicates that your child needs support and encouragement from you rather than harsh punishment.

When your child's behavior causes damage to people, relationships, and/or property, you should ensure that your child learns from his mistakes. An important part of the intervention process should focus on your child's experiencing biblical consequences for his misbehavior. If the injury is relational, your child should be held accountable for attempting to bring about reconciliation. If there is damage to property, your focus should be on your child's making restitution for what he has done. This kind of intervention will ensure that your child learns that there are measurable, practical consequences for misbehavior.

Unfortunately, in some instances your child may resent and resist any efforts you make to correct his misbehavior. Either he will refuse to do his part to bring about reconciliation, or he will fail to make restitution for the negative impact of his behavior. When a child actively or passively refuses to follow your directions and instructions, the child's behavior moves into the category of rebellion.

That kind of behavior usually puts your child and other people in some type of jeopardy. Impending rebellion calls for you to restate your expectations, repeat your instructions to your child so that you redirect his behavior, and warn him that failure to comply will result in serious consequences.

Rebellion on the part of your child warrants your implementing consequences for your child's misbehavior to minimize or stop the damage created by his actions and hopefully motivate your child to make the corrections necessary to be restored to a harmonious relationship with you. Failure to take corrective action could cripple your child's future, and it could also place you in a position of legal accountability that has serious consequences.[4]

When serious punishment is required, it is usually an indication that there is a lot of mental confusion and emotional unrest within your child. So proceed carefully. In order for your punitive action to reflect the required discipline of God, make an effort to address your child's unmet need so that you can settle his mental confusion and emotional unrest without compromising your expectation that he observe appropriate standards. Always administer punishment with sensitivity to the physical and emotional needs of your child. Punishment that does damage to the physical and emotional well-being of a child is outside the will of God (Colossians 3:21).

Translate your love for your child into intentional strategies to address his need

It is important that you take action that is appropriate to the behavior problem your child is experiencing. I recommend you take action using one of three different strategy levels.

LEVEL I: EARLY INTERVENTION STRATEGIES

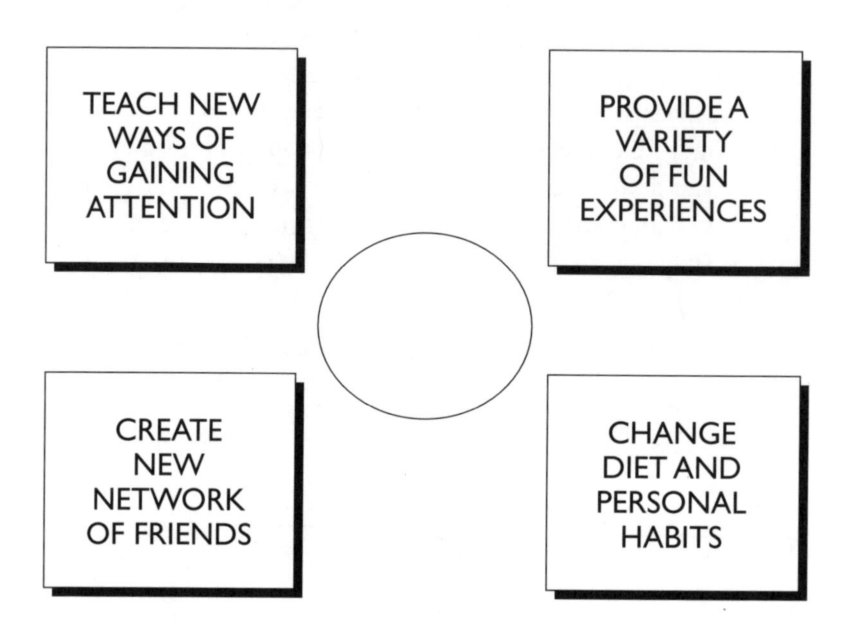

You should identify unhealthy patterns of independence and intervene early whenever possible.

LEVEL 2:
INTERMEDIATE INTERVENTION STRATEGIES

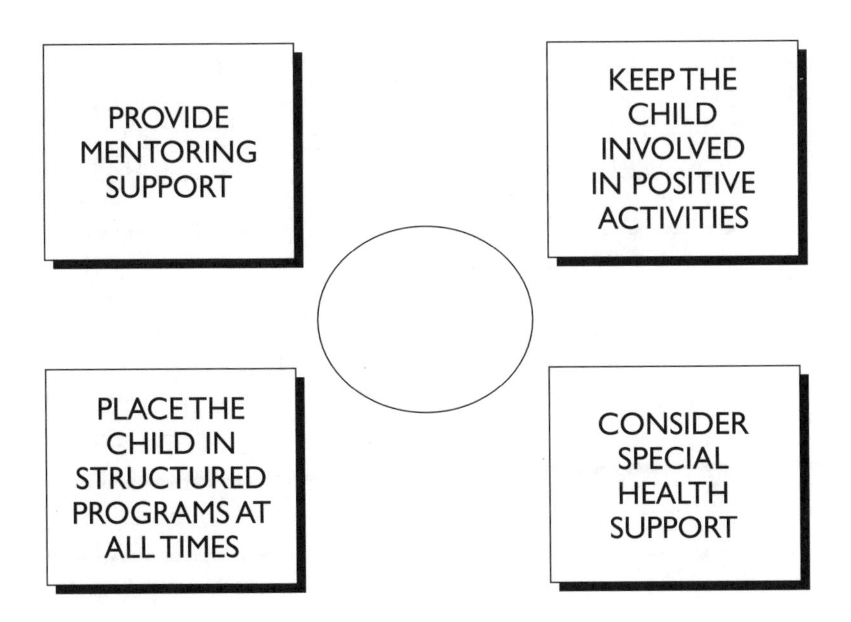

In some cases, the magnitude of the unhealthy behavior will require more aggressive intervention strategies.

LEVEL 3: CRISIS INTERVENTION STRATEGIES

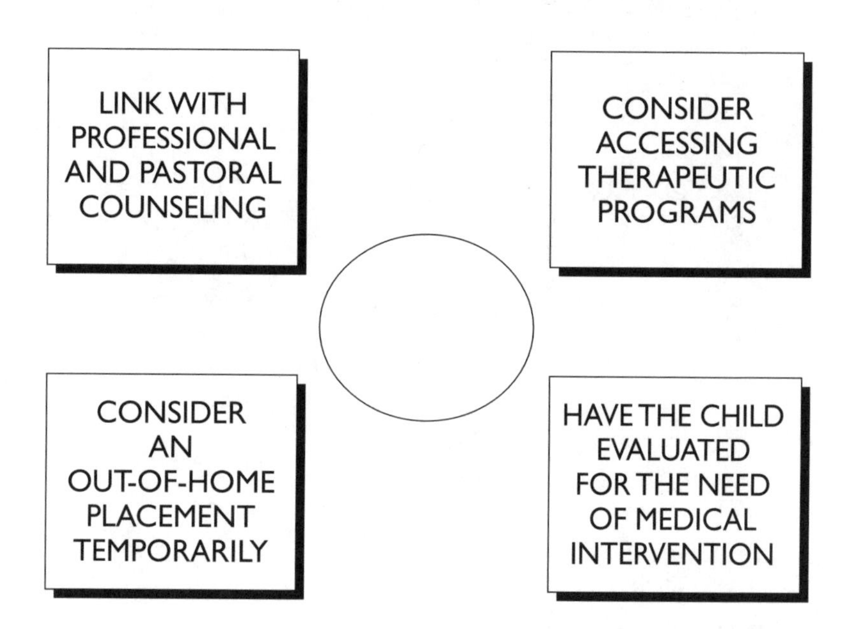

When your child or your family's well-being is seriously threatened, you should consider intervention strategies that are more intensive.

Take advantage of available resources and support

I have listed below a number of resources and strategies you may consider to help your child if he is experiencing special behavior problems.

ABC'S OF SUPPORT FOR PARENTS

All these activities and resources need to be evaluated to make sure they don't conflict in a harmful way with Christian principles and the personal values of your household.

Activities that enrich the lives of children
Behavioral health care organizations
Church-based and parachurch ministries
Dietary strategies and drug therapies
Educational programs
Friends and positive peer groups
Government sponsored programs
Hospital based programs
Independent social service agencies
Juvenile justice programs
Kinship network of support
Law enforcement agencies
Mental health professionals and organizations
Neighbors and community associations
Out-of-home placement programs
Professional counselors
Quality childcare and youth programs
Recreational programs
Structured supervision programs
Teachers and educational programs
University sponsored programs
Volunteer mentoring programs
Work opportunities
Xn (Christian education) programs
Youth service organizations
Zero tolerance standards

FAITH STEPS

1. Make sure your child's diet is free of substances and chemicals that negatively affect his behavior.

2. Give your child a sense of hope that the challenges of the present can be overcome in the future.

3. Build a positive peer support network for your child to help redirect his behavior in the right direction.

4. Structure your child's life experience so that you minimize the opportunities and options he has to engage in self-destructive behavior.

5. If you exceed your capacity to meet your child's needs and address his personal problems, seek pastoral and/or professional help.

A PARENT'S PRAYER

Father, Thank You for giving me the hope that any problems in my child's life are not greater than Your power. Keep my heart sensitive and responsive to my child's needs and not simply my own feelings. Help me to give my child the physical, emotional, social, and professional help he needs in times of crisis. Lead me to people, programs, and ministries that can help me meet the needs of my child in times of personal crisis. Amen.

PARENTING INSIGHTS

SPECIAL CARE INSTRUCTIONS

Research Highlight: The Threat of Addiction to Drugs and Alcohol

Addictions are real. Literally millions of people are enslaved to some form of addiction. These addictions could be related to sex, alcohol, drugs, food, and a number of other factors. Research points out some interesting aspects of addictions.[5] Although the implications cover a broad range of addictive behavior, this research highlight focuses most acutely on drugs and alcohol.

RESEARCH HIGHLIGHTS

- Examination of an addicted brain demonstrates that it is distinctively different physically and chemically from a normal brain.
- Alcohol and drug abuse "hijack" the brain, changing its motivational systems and how its genes function.[6]
- Alcohol abuse costs American citizens more than $185 billion in lost workdays and drunk driving accidents.
- Some 8 million Americans are addicted to alcohol, and 100,000 people die annually from alcohol-related causes.
- According to the Children of Alcoholics Foundation, children of alcoholics are four times more likely to become alcoholics than are children of nonalcoholics, and there are currently more than 6.6 million children of alcoholics under the age of eighteen in the United States.
- One survey estimated that by the time the average teenager is eighteen years old he will have witnessed more than 100,000 beer commercials on television.
- Some 2.4 million children have parents who are in prison, and more than 60 percent of their parents tested positive for substance abuse at the time of arrest. These children have a high statistical probability of becoming prisoners like their parents.

RESEARCH APPLICATIONS

1. Teach your child that alcohol should be considered a drug like other addictive substances.
2. Model a lifestyle that is not characterized by addictive behavior.
3. Filter out as many as you can of the promotions and advertisements trying to recruit your child to a lifetime of addiction.
4. Equip your child with the life skills necessary to respond to invitations and pressures to engage in behavior that will lead to addictions.
5. Stay informed about the kinds of drugs and substances that threaten the health and well-being of your child.
6. Encourage your child to surround himself with a peer group that is committed to avoiding addictive behavior.
7. Surround your child with activities and experiences that fill his life with pleasures that stimulate him in a healthy way and reduce his need for destructive sources of excitement.

"The teaching of the wise is a fountain of life, to turn aside from the snares of death" (Proverbs 13:14).

Every child wants to enjoy stimulation and pleasure. Your challenge is to fill your child's life with healthy, wholesome pleasures instead of destructive ones.

18

THE ULTIMATE STANDARD OF CARE

Faithfulness: God's Litmus Test

So where do you go from here? Well, I hope you have a renewed sense of privilege and purpose as a parent. Apart from your relationship with Jesus Christ, and your mate if you are married, there is no earthly gift more important than your child. Your child is "fearfully and wonderfully made."

You will probably have many jobs. You will probably live in a number of different homes. But God will give you only one opportunity to impact your child's life for eternity. Don't underestimate the importance of your role as a parent.

This child's life you will influence for eternity could be used by God to make a positive difference in the lives of countless people. That should give you a great sense of privilege. If you are not careful, the pressures and challenges of the role will crowd out the special opportunity you have as a parent to shape the life of your child.

But my prayer is that you have more than a sense of privilege. It is that you realize that God has provided you with the tools and resources you need to successfully help your child achieve God's purpose for her life. God's Word and the presence and power of the Holy Spirit will guide you to success if you display the spirit of love and commitment to doing what is in the best interests of your child.

If you are willing to work at it, when you stand before God and He asks you to give an account, your heart can say that you have been faithful. Your daily faithfulness will be your greatest expression of love and dedication to helping your child achieve God's purpose for her life.

After all, that is what God requires. He does not require perfection, just faithfulness. I hope this book has put your role as a parent into perspective for you. There is no such thing as a perfect parent. Even if you were a "perfect parent," that would not guarantee that you would have "perfect" children. Don't set a standard for yourself that even God has not set.

The Bible is a book filled with the stories of imperfect people. The opening chapters of the book of Genesis illustrate that the first two people God created chose evil over good in spite of having access to a perfect, loving God. Adam and Eve demonstrate to us that even though you have a perfect Father, struggles with daily choices will be there. Abraham was a precious servant of the Lord whom God promised to bless, yet he failed in many ways as a parent. Eli was clearly a man who loved God and the ministry, but he failed to give proper attention to the rearing of his children. The record of Scripture does not paint a picture that suggests there is a simple formula for problem-free parenting.

In fact, the Scriptures suggest just the opposite. It will be tough. Neither you nor your child will be exempt from the problems of obeying God on a daily basis. Failure is part of what causes you to run back to God asking for forgiveness and direction.

He knows we are imperfect, and His grace is greater than our limitations and failures. He loves us in spite of our imperfections. What a comfort! It gives me a great deal of peace to know that in spite of my imperfections as a parent, God still loves me.

Can I remind you that He loves you as much as I know He loves me? He loves you so much that His Son died on the cross for you. He loves you so much that even though you fail every day, His arms are open to extend love and forgiveness. That is incomprehensible love.

God wants us to love our children in the same way He loves us. That is the lifelong challenge. Unless God blesses you with an unusual child, you will sometimes struggle with your child's attitudes and actions. But you still need to love her anyway.

FAITH STEPS

What does God expect of you? He expects you to be faithful. I return to a simple set of suggestions made at the beginning of this book. Wake up every day with a commitment to these simple strategies:

1. Pray for your child every day.
2. Communicate spiritual truth to your child every day.
3. Encourage your child every day.
4. Provide for your child's unique needs every day.
5. Protect your child every day.
6. Model personal holiness for your child every day.
7. Promote responsibility in the life of your child every day.

Will you do this perfectly? No! You will win some parental struggles and lose some parental struggles. Some days you will feel like it happened just right. On other days you will want to quit. Expect the challenges.

But don't give up. Keep trying and trusting God. God will respond to your prayers and cries for help. If you apply the principles from Scripture to your parenting responsibility, God will honor your efforts. After all, your child is *a gift from God.*

A PARENT'S PRAYER

Father, Thank You for calling me to be a parent. Help me to remember that my child is a gift from You. Help me to recognize the uniqueness of my child, and guide her to fulfill her purpose for her life. Focus my thoughts and actions on Your Word as my source of authority and wisdom. Allow me to follow the leading of Your Spirit as I make daily parenting decisions. When my child fails, give me a spirit of mercy and grace. Keep my mind directed toward the needs of my child as the passion of my heart and parental decisions. Grant me the favor to stand before You and hear Your acknowledgement of my faithfulness as a parent. May I return to You a child who has enjoyed the privilege of a life well lived and whose desire is to offer her life in service to Jesus Christ in whatever way, whatever role, whatever place You ordain. Amen.

PARENTING INSIGHTS

SPECIAL CARE INSTRUCTIONS

Research Highlight: The Church as Part of Your Child's Support System

Groundbreaking research by The Search Institute measured assets in more than 100,000 American youths. The Institute found that the presence of forty key assets were a powerful protection against serious behavior problems and showed that a local congregation of believers can play a critical role in the success of youth.[1]

RESEARCH HIGHLIGHTS

- Twenty assets identified by the Search Institute must come from outside the young person. Twenty internal assets develop inside the young person.
- The external assets include support, empowerment, boundaries and expectations, and constructive use of time. The internal assets include commitment to learning, positive values, social competencies, and a positive identity.
- Youth who have all forty of the developmental assets are 30 percent less likely to be involved in sexual activity, 55 percent less likely to get involved in violence, 50 percent less likely to have problems with alcohol, 46 percent more likely to be successful in school, 63 percent more likely to maintain good health, and 25 percent more likely to help others than youths of the same age who had from one to ten of the assets.
- A local church can effectively play a pivotal role in the life of a young person who comes from a difficult family situation by compensating for assets that the child's parents don't provide.
- The research concluded that many "faith communities" are already committed to addressing the well-being youth and that asset building is a "natural expression of their commitments."
- Congregations already provide a place of spiritual instruction, a

supportive community of accountability and support, and involve their youth in regular service projects.

RESEARCH APPLICATIONS

1. Make your personal involvement in the ministry of a local church a high priority.
2. Cultivate in your child a passion to learn the Scriptures as the foundation for developing a value system. Shape character through home-based instruction and participation in church-based growth experiences. Keep your child involved in learning, growing, and serving as a part of the ministry of your local church.
3. Allow your child to participate in "transformational experiences," such as vacation Bible schools, camps, and other events sponsored by your local church.
4. Model service to Christ through the ministry of your local church and other parts of the body of Christ.
5. Ask committed members of your local church to provide an extended source of accountability and support for your child.
6. Foster involvement in service opportunities by your child in church and community projects that minister to the needs of other people.

"We will not conceal them from their children, but tell to the generation to come the praises of the Lord, and his strength and His wondrous works that He has done" (Psalm 78:4).

Surround your child with people who love her and will encourage her to do her best.

Appendix A

USING BIBLICAL PRINCIPLES TO GUIDE YOUR PARENTING PRACTICES

Can I share a dream with you? Throughout the book we gave you much information. Some of the information came from personal experiences. Very important research findings were discussed also. And I hope you noticed that all of the principles were anchored in Scripture.

That's where my dream comes in. I dream that you will embrace the principles from Scripture more than anything else you have read. Why?

The personal experiences I have related may bring the principles alive, but they are not authoritative. Applying research findings may be helpful, but they are often limited by time, circumstances, and, sometimes, economic resources. The Scripture, though, transcends culture, class, ethnicity, economic status, and educational level. It meets us all where we live. You could say the Bible is the great parenting equalizer.

I acknowledge that there is not a completely developed systematic theology in the Scriptures about the process a child moves through from conception to maturity, nor is there one for the parenting process. But the Bible is not silent. The general teachings of the Bible lay the foundation for significant observations about children and their development.

This appendix is designed to get you started on a lifelong journey of thinking through your parenting responsibilities with the Scriptures in your hand and honoring God on your mind. I have chosen a few sample verses to illustrate how you can think through these ideas.

Some of these passages address children directly, and some of them have indirect application to the growth and maturity of your child or the parenting process. This appendix will give you an opportunity to reflect on your current parenting practices in light of what the Scripture teaches.

Take the time to reflect on these principles and ask God to help you develop a biblical approach to parenting. By the way, this is not an overnight process. Relax. Start by making the decision you want to start the journey.

It may even seem like a really long journey depending on where you are starting. But it will be well worth the effort. My suggestion to you is that you take the time to answer the questions after you review each principle. You may even decide to create a journal for yourself to track your personal progress.

It may be a good idea to discuss this journey with your mate or a very close friend with whom you can enter into an accountability relationship over a period of time. This may help you stay on the journey when the crush of life starts robbing you of energy and time.

The purpose of this appendix is not really to evaluate where you are when you begin the process of adapting your parenting practices to biblical principles. The real question is where you are over a period of time after you have bathed your passion to parent biblically in prayer and meditated over how God wants you to apply these principles. Maybe you could make developing a biblical parenting style a personal project for the next twelve months.

So how do you get started? What passages should you look at? What should you do with the passages? Let me give you a few instructions and illustrations to get you started.

TRANSFERABLE BIBLICAL PRINCIPLES AND OBSERVATIONS

There are a number of passages we could examine from the Bible to develop a set of guiding principles for your parenting. Twelve specific passages of Scripture were chosen to illustrate the relevance of the Bible to your mission and everyday responsibilities as a parent. We will ask three questions of the Scripture when we develop these applications

What does the Scripture say?

What does it mean?

What difference should it make in my parenting practices?

A very simple pattern will be followed with each of the three passages we have chosen. We will state a parental application, share a parenting principle from the text of Scripture, and then make some observations that will help you apply the principle to your daily parenting activities. The goal is to launch you on a journey of personal study of the Scriptures so that you can develop a biblical literacy that will give you greater confidence in your parenting.

Let's look at a few observations from Scripture.

1
Your child is a gift from God to you.

Behold, children are a gift of the Lord, the fruit of the womb is a reward. (Psalm 127:3)

Parental Principle: Every child is a gift from God, and a mother should consider children a reward from God.

Observations: Sometimes the pressures of life cause us to lose sight of the fact that God gives children to parents. We all need to keep our perspective focused on the fact that our child did not come by accident, but by the providential plan of God.

You and I have the challenge of constantly reminding ourselves of this spiritual principle when life gets hard. For personal growth, take the time to reflect on your attitude and practice as a parent to your child.

Parental Reflection: Do I treat my child like a gift from God?

1 2 3 4 5 6 7 8 9 10

Never *Sometimes* *Often* *Most of the Time* *Almost Always*

2
Your child has a special mission from God.

Your eyes have seen my unformed substance; and in Your book were all written the days that were ordained for me, when as yet there was not one of them. (Psalm 139:16)

Parental Principle: God knows every person intimately from the time she is in her mother's womb, and He has a special mission for every child's life.

Observations: You have the opportunity to communicate to your child that God has a unique purpose and design for her life. This means you have to first feel that way in your heart. Then you can spend the rest of your life as a parent communicating this simple but profound spiritual truth to your child.

Parental Reflection: Do I communicate to my child that God has a special plan for her life?

1	2	3	4	5	6	7	8	9	10
	Never		*Sometimes*		*Often*		*Most of the Time*		*Almost Always*

3
Your child needs personalized guidance from you so he can find God's purpose for his life.

Train up child in the way he should go, even when he is old he will not depart from it. (Proverbs 22:6)

Parental Principle: A parent should guide every child's life so he pursues the unique pattern and/or blueprint God has for his life, with the result that the child will ultimately not depart from God's design for his life.

Observations: You have the opportunity to help your child discover God's unique purpose and design for his life. This means that a significant part of your personal energy should be focused on being a student of the unique characteristics and qualities your child has been given by God.

As you identify the unique ways God has built your child, you can give him the counsel, instruction, experiences that will guide him in the way you believe God wants him to go. There is no indication in the Scripture that this will be an easy and pain-free process for any parent. But even if it is very difficult, you should try your best to help your child respond to God's call and direction for his life.

Parental Reflection: Am I helping my child discover God's unique purpose for his life?

1 2 3 4 5 6 7 8 9 10

Never *Sometimes* *Often* *Most of the Time* *Almost Always*

4
A mother has the opportunity to pass her personal faith on to her child.

For I am mindful of the sincere faith within you, which first dwelt in your grandmother Lois, and your mother Eunice, and I am sure that it is in you as well. (2 Timothy 1:5)

Parental Principle: Motherhood creates a special opportunity to transmit faith from one generation to the next.

Observations: Normally, a mother spends the greatest amount of time with a child during the first few years of the child's life. This creates a special opportunity for transmitting personal faith to her child.

This unique opportunity to shape a child's life during the early window when she grows so much and so fast, along with the lifetime platform a mother has, should be taken very seriously. Every day should be seen as a chance to teach children how to love God through sensitive care by the mother. Giving her child nurture and love will create a wonderful platform to help the child embrace God's love later.

Parental Reflection: Does my child have the opportunity to benefit from the nurturing presence of a mother who loves her and cares for her personal needs?

1 2 3 4 5 6 7 8 9 10

Never *Sometimes* *Often* *Most of the Time* *Almost Always*

5
You should create an environment for your child that allows you to teach him about God through formal and informal experiences as a part of your daily routine.

"Hear, O Israel! The Lord is our God, the Lord is one! You shall love the Lord your God with all your heart and with all your soul and with all your might. These words, which I am commanding you today, shall be on your heart. You shall teach them diligently to your sons and shall talk of them when you sit in your house and when you walk by the way and when you lie down and when you rise up. You shall bind them as a sign on your hand and they shall be as frontals on your forehead. You shall write them on the doorposts of your house and on your gates." (Deuteronomy 6:4–9)

Parental Principle: A believing parent has a special responsibility to pass on his faith to his children through sights, sounds, and symbols in the household and through personal routines that honor God.

Observations: You should consciously shape the art, music, and practices in your contact with your child to help him learn the principles of Scripture and to follow the example of your life.

If you find a way to weave learning to love and follow God into the routines of your personal life, your child will be less likely to see his faith in God as simply religious expression. He is more likely to develop a personal understanding of what it means to have a relationship with a living, personal God.

Parental Reflection: Am I using each of my everyday life experiences to teach my child spiritual truth?

1 2 3 4 5 6 7 8 9 10

Never *Sometimes* *Often* *Most of the Time* *Almost Always*

6

Fathers have an opportunity to shape the spiritual development of their children by bringing them up with an understanding of God's principles for living.

Fathers, do not provoke your children to anger, but bring them up in the discipline and instruction of the Lord. (Ephesians 6:4)

Parental Principle: Fathers have a personal obligation to teach their children how to live in accordance with the teaching of the Scripture.

Observation: Every father has an opportunity to use his platform to teach his children the principles of Scripture through the daily relationships of life. Fathers need to be very serious about not relegating their responsibility to teach their children to others, but rather to see themselves as the primary shapers of the character of their children.

Parental Reflection: Does my child have access to a strong father figure to model for and teach her how to live according to the teaching of Scripture?

1 2 3 4 5 6 7 8 9 10

Never *Sometimes* *Often* *Most of the Time* *Almost Always*

7
Your child should be expected to honor your parental authority.

"Honor your father and your mother, that your days may be prolonged in the land which the Lord your God gives you." (Exodus 20:12)

Parental Principle: Every child should be expected to honor parental authority.

Observation: You should make sure you help your child learn to respect authority in the home so he can transfer that respect to adults outside of the home. If your child does not learn to respond to your authority in the home, it will be even more difficult for him to learn to respect other adults outside of the home. This is an important contribution you can make to the life of your child.

The Bible clearly teaches that your child's life span will be greatly enhanced if he learns to respond properly to authority. You could literally extend your child's life by teaching him to respect and honor boundaries. Take this responsibility very seriously.

Parental Reflection: Am I teaching my child to respect my parental authority?

1	2	3	4	5	6	7	8	9	10
	Never		*Sometimes*		*Often*		*Most of the Time*		*Almost Always*

8
You should correct your child with sensitivity and grace so that she can develop a righteous life.

But if you are without discipline, of which all have become partakers, then you are illegitimate children and not sons. Furthermore, we had earthly fathers to discipline us, and we respected them; shall we not much rather be subject to the Father of spirits, and live? For they disciplined us for a short time as seemed best to them, but He disciplines us for our good, so that we may share His holiness. All discipline for the moment seems not to be joyful, but sorrowful; yet to those who have been trained by it, afterwards it yields the peaceful fruit of righteousness. (Hebrews 12:8–11)

Parental Principle: Children should be disciplined in a loving, effective manner so that they can develop righteous lives.

Observation: Since your child will sometimes fail to live up to your expectations, you have the opportunity to correct her and get her back on track through loving discipline. In fact, the greatest expression of your love for your child will sometimes be expressed through your willingness to stop her when she is off track and teach her how to honor God.

It is sometimes hard to establish boundaries for children when you feel they may reject you. But you must. If you keep focused, it can result in the peaceful fruit of righteousness.

Parental Reflection: Am I cultivating righteousness in the life of my child through effective discipline?

1	2	3	4	5	6	7	8	9	10
	Never		*Sometimes*		*Often*		*Most of the Time*		*Almost Always*

9
Your child should not be treated so harshly that it causes him to lose heart.

Fathers, do not exasperate your children, so that they will not lose heart. (Colossians 3:21)

Parental Principle: Every child should be treated with sensitivity by his parents, especially his father, so that he will not lose heart. It is possible for a parent, especially a father, to engage in behavior that is destructive to a child's emotional well-being.

Observation: Here is where you have to be very sensitive. It is possible for you to respond to your child's misbehavior in a manner that is destructive. That is why it is so important for you to be careful about how you correct your child when you administer discipline.

It is really simple—if you are angry at your child and are tempted to do things that intentionally hurt him, then you need to stop and ask God to calm you down. When a child loses heart it keeps him from growing and living up to his God-given potential.

One of the greatest gifts you can give your child is a sense of worth before God. Be careful. Handle your child's emotional state with care.

Parental Reflection: Do I show sensitivity to my child's emotional well-being when I discipline him?

1	2	3	4	5	6	7	8	9	10
	Never		*Sometimes*		*Often*		*Most of the Time*		*Almost Always*

10
You should learn to hold your child accountable yet love her even when she fails to live up to your expectations until she comes back home.

"So he got up and came to his father. But while he was still a long way off, his father saw him and felt compassion for him, and ran and embraced him and kissed him. And the son said to him, 'Father, I have sinned against heaven and in your sight; I am no longer worthy to be called your son.' But the father said to his slaves, 'Quickly bring out the best robe and put it on him, and put a ring on his hand and sandals on his feet; and bring the fattened calf, kill it, and let us eat and celebrate." (Luke 15:20–23)

Parental Principle: A parent should hold his child accountable but not give up on her when she fails.

Observations: There will be times when your child will fail to live up to your expectations. You have to choose between several options.

- You could simply give up and let her do whatever she wants without consequences.
- You could reject her without any compassion for her.
- You could let her experience the consequences of her actions with a spirit of compassion toward her and expectancy of her repentance.

The Scripture gives a beautiful picture of compassionate accountability by a loving father that you and I can imitate with our children.

Parental Reflection: Do I handle my child's failures with compassionate accountability?

1	2	3	4	5	6	7	8	9	10
	Never		*Sometimes*		*Often*		*Most of the Time*		*Almost Always*

11

You should allow the community of believers God has surrounded you with to support your ministry to your child.

Listen, O my people, to my instruction; incline your ears to the words of my mouth. I will open my mouth in a parable; I will utter dark sayings of old, which we have heard and known, and our fathers have told us. We will not conceal them from their children, but tell to the generations to come the praises of the Lord, and His wondrous works that He has done. (Psalm 78:1–4)

Parental Principle: God expects believers to share stories of His faithfulness to children across generations and family lines.

Observations: Since God has challenged the community of believers to support each other with the development of children, you should take full advantage of the network of support already around you. If a support group of believers is not readily available, consider whether God wants you to develop such a network.

God never intended for anyone of us to assume the full weight and challenge of parenting alone. Take advantage of the support of other believers who share your values. Let them be an additional voice to support you in your efforts to parent your children.

Parental Reflection: Do I allow my child to take in the life lessons and experiences of the community of believers God has provided for our family?

1 2 3 4 5 6 7 8 9 10

Never *Sometimes* *Often* *Most of the Time* *Almost Always*

12
You should give your child a foundation of wisdom that can lead her to a personal relationship with God and training in righteousness.

You, however, continue in the things you have learned and become convinced of, knowing from whom you have learned them, and that from childhood you have known the sacred writings which are able to give you the wisdom that leads to salvation through faith which is in Christ Jesus. All Scripture is inspired by God and profitable for teaching, for reproof, for correction, for training in righteousness. (2 Timothy 3:14–16)

Parental Principle: God has given us His Word as the foundation for guiding our children to develop a personal relationship with Jesus Christ and live a fruitful Christian life.

Observations: Giving your child a strong biblical foundation during the early years of her life could serve her for eternity. If you give your child the foundation of Scripture she will have a source of truth that can address her life circumstances in a comprehensive manner.

She may not appreciate your teaching until later in her life, but this verse is a wonderful affirmation that God's Word is alive and active and can play a profound role in your life and the life of your child. Don't give up. Keep presenting God's Word to your child and let God take care of the results.

Parental Reflection: Am I guiding my child to learn the principles of biblical wisdom that can lead her to salvation and help her live a fruitful life?

1	2	3	4	5	6	7	8	9	10
	Never		*Sometimes*		*Often*		*Most of the Time*		*Almost Always*

CONCLUSION

This list has not been exhaustive, but it hopefully has been illustrative. The Bible is filled with other principles you can use to help you teach your children. You have a wonderful resource in God's Word right at your fingertips.

Now the challenge to you is get started and take one day at a time.

You can use the Bible as your primary reference tool for teaching and developing your children. Since your child is the greatest gift God can possibly give, you have the opportunity to use the greatest book that has ever been written to help develop this wonderful gift from God.

Appendix B

A PRAYER JOURNEY USING THE BOOK OF PROVERBS

So how do you intelligently pray for your children? There are many ways you can pray for your children—even using the Scripture as your guide. The book of Proverbs is filled with wisdom you can give your children to help them navigate through life successfully. Using this journey through the book of Proverbs as a prayer guide will help you focus your conversations with God about your children and even impact the way you interact with them on a daily basis.

1. **Willingness to Listen**

   "Hear, my son, your father's instruction and do not forsake your mother's teaching; indeed, they are a graceful wreath to your head and ornaments about your neck" (Proverbs 1:8–9).

   Lord, please enable our children to develop a willingness to listen to our instruction as parents.

2. **Heart of Wisdom**
   "My son, if you will receive my words and treasure my commandments within you, make your ear attentive to wisdom, incline your heart to understanding; for if you cry for discernment, lift your voice for understanding; if you seek her as silver and search for her as for hidden treasures; then you will discern the fear of the Lord and discover the knowledge of God (Proverbs 2:1–5).

   Father, give my children a heart of wisdom so they can discern right from wrong as they make their daily decisions.

3. **Trust in the Lord**
   "Trust in the Lord with all your heart and do not lean on your own understanding. In all your ways acknowledge Him, and He will make your paths straight" (Proverbs 3:5–6).

   I pray that my children will trust in You, instead of themselves, as they are faced with difficult decisions.

4. **Resistance to Negative People**
   "Do not enter the path of the wicked and do not proceed in the way of evil men. Avoid it, do not pass by it; turn away from it and pass on" (Proverbs 4:14–15).

   Keep my children from the path of negative people as they go to school, play, and work in the neighborhood.

5. **Sexual Purity**
   "For why should you, my son, be exhilarated with an adulteress and embrace the bosom of a foreigner? For the ways of a man are before the eyes of the Lord, and He watches all his paths" (Proverbs 5:20–21).

   Please give me the insight I need to help my children maintain sexual purity in spite of all the temptations they will face.

6. **Honesty**
"A worthless person, a wicked man, is the one who walks with a perverse mouth, who winks with his eyes, who signals with his feet, who points with his fingers; who with perversity in his heart continually devises evil, who spreads strife. Therefore his calamity will come suddenly; instantly he will be broken and there will be no healing" (Proverbs 6:12–15).

   Lord, may my children walk with integrity and demonstrate honesty in all their activities and relationships.

7. **Resistance to Evil Women**
"And behold, a woman comes to meet him, dressed as a harlot and cunning of heart. She is boisterous and rebellious, her feet do not remain at home; she is now in the streets, now in the squares, and lurks by every corner" (Proverbs 7:10–12).

   Father, give my children the strength to resist temptations from people who seek to seduce and direct them toward evil.

8. **Way of Righteousness**
"I walk in the way of righteousness, in the midst of the paths of justice, to endow those who love me with wealth, that I may fill their treasuries" (Proverbs 8:20–21).

   Lord, please guide my children so that they walk in the way of righteousness as a regular part of their lives.

9. **Teachable Attitude**
"Give instruction to a wise man and he will be still wiser, teach a righteous man and he will increase his learning" (Proverbs 9:9).

   Father, keep my children's minds open to learning wisdom that comes from You so that they have a teachable attitude.

10. Willingness to Work

"Poor is he who works with a negligent hand, but the hand of the diligent makes rich. He who gathers in summer is a son who acts wisely, but he who sleeps in harvest is a son who acts shamefully" (Proverbs 10:4–5).

Keep my children from an attitude of laziness; help them maintain a commitment to work and handle their tasks diligently.

11. Personal Counselors

"Where there is no guidance the people fall, but in abundance of counselors there is victory" (Proverbs 11:14).

Give my children counselors who will help them make good personal decisions so that they will not experience many unnecessary personal falls.

12. High Esteem

"Better is he who is lightly esteemed and has a servant than he who honors himself and lacks bread" (Proverbs 12:9).

Let my children be held in high esteem by their peers, teachers, counselors, and other people they interact with.

13. Heart free of Anxiety

"Hope deferred makes the heart sick, but desire fulfilled is a tree of life" (Proverbs 13:12).

Please keep my children free from a heart of anxiety.

14. Slow to Anger

"He who is slow to anger has great understanding, but he who is quick-tempered exalts folly" (Proverbs 14:29).

Allow my children to develop the capacity to control their anger and keep their temper in times of stress.

15. Soothing Tongue

"A soothing tongue is a tree of life, but perversion in it crushes the spirit" (Proverbs 15:4).

Help my children use their tongues to give life to other people and avoid crushing the spirit of their peers.

16. Humility

"Pride goes before destruction, and a haughty spirit before stumbling. It is better to be humble in spirit with the lowly than to divide the spoil with the proud" (Proverbs 16:18–19).

Keep my children free from a spirit of pride and give them an attitude of humility.

17. Cheerful Heart

"A joyful heart is good medicine, but a broken spirit dries up the bones" (Proverbs 17:22).

Fill my children's lives with the kinds of activities that will help them maintain a cheerful heart in the face of all the negative peers and circumstances they will face.

18. Sustaining Friendships

"A man of too many friends comes to ruin, but there is a friend who sticks closer than a brother" (Proverbs 18:24).

Give my children a few sustaining friendships so that when they feel rejected and misunderstood, they will not feel like they are totally alone.

19. Respect for Parents

"He who assaults his father and drives his mother away is a shameful and disgraceful son. Cease listening, my son, to discipline, and you will stray from the words of knowledge" (Proverbs 19:26–27).

Help my children maintain a proper respect for me as a parent and the one responsible for caring for their needs.

20. Distinctive Life

"It is by his deeds that a lad distinguishes himself if his conduct is pure and right" (Proverbs 20:11).

Keep my children's lives distinctive in the view of their peers, teachers, and other adults.

21. Commitment to Justice

"The exercise of justice is joy for the righteous, but is terror to the workers of iniquity" (Proverbs 21:15).

Direct my children's actions so they interact with their siblings and friends in a just way.

22. Fulfillment of God's Purpose

"Train up a child in the way he should go, even when he is old he will not depart from it" (Proverbs 22:6).

Enable me to guide my children so they achieve Your purpose for their lives.

23. Freedom from Revelers

"Do not be with heavy drinkers of wine, or with gluttonous eaters of meat; for the heavy drinker and the glutton will come to poverty, and drowsiness will clothe one with rags" (Proverbs 23:20–21).

When people who are a negative influence on my children come around, give my children the courage to stay away.

24. Personal Responsibility

"I passed by the field of the sluggard and by the vineyard of the man lacking sense, and behold, it was completely overgrown with thistles; its surface was covered with nettles, and its stone wall was broken down. When I saw, I reflected upon it; I looked, and received instruction. 'A little sleep, a little slumber, a little folding of the hands to rest,' then your poverty will come as a robber and your want like an armed man" (Proverbs 24:30–34).

Make everyday responsibility in the lives of my children a pattern that helps them become responsible adults.

25. Self-Control

"Like a city that is broken into and without walls is a man who has no control over his spirit" (Proverbs 25:28).

Strengthen my children so that they can keep control of their emotions through the ebbs and flows of the circumstances of their lives.

26. Ability to Learn from Their Mistakes

"Like a dog that returns to its vomit is a fool who repeats his folly" (Proverbs 26:11).

Prevent my children from repeating their mistakes by giving them the ability to learn from their mistakes.

27. Discernment to Avoid Evil

"A prudent man sees evil and hides himself, the naïve proceed and pay the penalty" (Proverbs 27:12).

Open my children's eyes to see the evil all around them and give them the discernment they need to avoid the problems that will befall.

28. A Clean Heart

"He who conceals his transgressions will not prosper, but he who confesses and forsakes them will find compassion" (Proverbs 28:13).

Guard my children so that they keep their hearts pure and confess their sins as You bring them to their attention.

29. Concern for the Rights of Poor

"The righteous is concerned for the rights of the poor, the wicked does not understand such concern" (Proverbs 29:7).

Open my children's hearts to respond to the rights of those who don't have someone else speaking for them.

30. Self-restraint

"If you have been foolish in exalting yourself or if you have plotted evil, put your hand on your mouth" (Proverbs 30:32).

Cause my children to use personal restraint when they begin to place too much attention on themselves or plan to do evil.

31. Commitment to Honor Their Mother

"Her children rise up and bless her; her husband also, and he praises her, saying, 'Many daughters have done nobly, but you excel them all.'" (Proverbs 31:28–29).

Give my children the sensitivity and confidence to affirm the work of their mother and honor her for all her support and sacrifice.

You could use this guide as a regular part of your daily time of prayer with the Lord. If you miss a day for some reason, just pick up on the next day where you left off. You don't have to be intimidated or feel locked into doing this process perfectly. It can be a tool you use as a resource to help you with the stewardship of your children as you guide them from childhood to adulthood.

NOTES

Chapter 1: On Loan from God: Steward of Divine Life

1. Mamie Gene Cole, "I Am the Child," in Cynthia Pearl Maus, *Christ and the Fine Arts* (New York: Harper & Row, 1959), 28.
2. Joan Raymond, "The World of the Senses," *Newsweek,* Fall/Winter 2000, 16–18.
3. Stephen P. Williams, "The New Face of Nutrition," *Newsweek,* Fall/Winter, 42–45.

Chapter 2: By Divine Design: Discover and Encourage Your Child's Uniqueness

1. Bob Foltman, " Venus in Own Orbit," *Chicago Tribune,* Chicago Sports Final, 19 January 2001.
2. William J. Bennet, *The Book of Virtues* (New York: Simon & Schuster, 1996), 386–87. All rights reserved.
3. See the Web site published by the National Information Center for Children and Youth with Disabilities On-line: http://www.nichcy.org.
4. "General Information About Disabilities," National Information Center for Children and Youth with Disabilities On-line: http://www.nichcy.org.
5. See Sharon Begley, "Wired for Thought," *Newsweek* Special Edition, Fall/Winter 2000; and David L. Marcus, Anna Mulrine, and Kathleen Wong, "How Kids Learn," *U.S. News & World Report,* 11September 1999, 44–52.

Chapter 3: Fragile: Handle with Care: Nurturing Your Child's Emotional Temperament

1. Jill Riethmayer, "Trauma's Youngest Victims: The Children," *Christian Counseling Today* 7, no. 1 (1999): 32–35.

Chapter 4: Seek Long-term Insurance: Meeting Your Child's Spiritual Needs

1. Edgar Guest, "Sermons We See," in Clyde Francis Lytle, ed., *Leaves of Gold* (Fort Worth, Tex.: Brownlow), 9.
2. Mary Ann Davies, "Learning . . . The Beat Goes On," *Childhood Education,* Spring 2000, 148–52.

Chapter 5: Heavenly Specifications: Your Child's Growth and Development

1. Dr. Michael D. Jacobson, *The Word on Health* (Chicago: Moody, 2000), 70–76.
2. Daniel Goleman, *Emotional Intelligence* (New York: Bantam, 1995).
3. Judy Slays, "Principles of Godly Health Maintenance," *The Teaching Home,* July/August 1999, 35–37.
4. Geoffrey Cowley, "Generation Fat," *Newsweek,* 3 July 2000, 40–44.
5. Linda Avallone, "Seven Steps to Teaching Nutrition," *The Teaching Home,* July/August 1999, 38.

Chapter 6: Power Source: Strength for Biblical Parenting

1. David L Marcus, Anna Mulrine, and Kathleen Wong, "How Kids Learn," *U.S. News & World Report,* 11 September 1999, 44–52.

Chapter 7: The Instruction Manual: Role of Scripture in Your Parenting

1. Harry Shields and Gary Bredfeldt, *Caring for Souls: Counseling Under the Authority of Scripture* (Chicago: Moody, 2001), 37–38.
2. Josh McDowell, *Evidence that Demands a Verdict,* Arrowhead Springs, Calif.: Campus Crusade, 1972), 18.
3. Barna Research Online, "The Bible," a research archive, and "Americans' Knowledge Is in the Ballpark, but Often Off Base" (12 July 2000), both at http://www.barna.org.

Chapter 8: Special Delivery: The Importance of a Godly Mother

1. Franklin Graham, *Rebel with a Cause* (Nashville: Thomas Nelson, 1995), 19–20.
2. Lindsey O'Connor, "Moms Who Changed the World," *Single-Parent Family,* May 2000, 14–16.
3. See Shannon Brownlee, "Baby Talk," *U.S. News & World Report,* 15 June 1998, 48–55.

Chapter 9: God's Security System: The Father's Influence on a Child's Life

1. Joseph P. Shapiro, Joannie M. Schrof, Mike Tharp, and Dorian Friedman, "Honor Thy Children," *U.S. News & World Report,* 27 February 1995, 38–49.
2. Dan Malone, "Crimes of the Father: Son Placed for Adoption Follows His Parent to Death Row," *Dallas Morning News,* 20 October 1997, 1A.
3. See Gary Oliver, "The War on Boys," *New Man,* November/December 2000, 48–55.

Chapter 10: Wrap in Righteousness: The Christian Home: God's Platform for Developing Character

1. See Walter Kirn, "Should You Stay Together for the Kids?" *Time,* 25 September 2000, 75–82.

Chapter 11: Use Memory Power: Teaching Your Child through Life Experiences

1. See Marlene Magdar, "Online for Trouble," *Christian Counseling Today* 8, no. 3 (Summer 2000): 32–34; and Daniel Okrent, "Raising Kids Online: What Can Parents Do?" *Time,* 10 May 1999, 38–40.

Chapter 12: Keep in Safe Places: Monitoring Social Influences on Your Child's Life

1. See Herbert L. Needleman and Phillip J. Landrigan, *Raising Children Toxic Free* (New York: Avon, 1994), 17–26; and Claudia Kalb, "Keeping Your Child Safe," *Newsweek* Special Issue, Fall/Winter 2000, 38–41.

Chapter 13: Warning: Keep Away from Danger: Protecting Your Child from Danger

1. Archibald D. Hart, *Stress and Your Child: Know the Signs and Prevent the Harm* (Waco, Tex.: Word, 1992), 6–10.
2. Paula Rinehart, "Losing Our Promiscuity," *Christianity Today,* 10 July 2000, 35.
3. Annie E. Casey Online: http://www.aecf.org/kidscount/teen/ "When Teens Have Sex: Issues and Trends," A KIDS COUNT Special Report.
4. Rinehart, "Losing Our Promiscuity," 38.
5. Jerry Johnston, *It's Killing Our Kids: the Growing Epidemic of Teenage Alcohol Abuse and Addiction* (Waco, Tex.: Word, 1991), xv–xviii.
6. Susan A. Miller, "Family Television Viewing—How to Gain Control," *Childhood Education,* Fall 1997, 38–41.
7. Kerby Anderson, "Coping with Violence in Contemporary Society," in *The Christian Educator's Handbook on Family Life Education,* edited by Kenneth O. Gangel and James C. Wilhoit (Grand Rapids: Baker, 1996), 255–68.
8. Ibid.
9. Mary C. Turck, *A Parent's Guide to the Best Children's Videos and Where to Find Them* (New York: Houghton Mifflin, 1994), 3.
10. Kenneth Wooden, *Child Lures* (Arlington, Tex.: Summit Group, 1995), xi.
11. Matthew D. Frey, "Learning from Littleton," *Baptist Bulletin,* June 1999, 8–10.
12. See Anderson, "Coping with Violence in Contemporary Society," in *The Christian Educator's Handbook on Family Life Education,* 255–68.

Chapter 14: Troubleshooting: Discipline from a Biblical Perspective

1. "What Is Childhood Maltreatment?" July 2000 posting, National Clearinghouse on Child Abuse and Neglect Information.
2. "Child Abuse and Neglect National Statistics," April 2000 posting, National Clearinghouse on Child Abuse and Neglect Information, summarizing highlights of a U.S. Department of Health

and Human Services report, *Child Maltreatment 1998: Reports from the States to the National Child Abuse and Neglect Data System* (Washington, D.C.: U.S. Government Printing Office).

3. Ibid.

Chapter 15: Prescription for Brokenness: When Your Child Strays

1. See Paula Rinehart, "Losing Our Promiscuity," *Christianity Today,* 10 July 2000, 32–39.

Chapter 16: No Returns Accepted: Handling the Struggle of Caring for Your Child

1. See National Information Center for Children and Youth with Disabilities On-line: http://www.nichcy.org.

Chapter 17: Dealing with Emergencies: Addressing Serious Behavior Problems

1. Stephen Larson, "Meeting the Needs of Youthful Offenders through the Spiritual Dimension," *Reclaiming Children and Youth,* vol. 5, no. 3 (1996): 167–72.
2. Francisco Contreras, "Better Health: Better You," *Profile* 10 (February/March 2000): 26–31.
3. Howard Egan-Chua, "Escaping from the Darkness," *Time,* 31 May 1999, 44–49.
4. D. L. Forman, *Every Parent's Guide to the Law* (San Diego: Harcourt Brace, 1998).
5. Jonathan Alter, "The War on Addiction," *Newsweek,* 12 February 2001, 37–39.
6. Sharon Begley, "How it all Starts Inside Your Brain," *Newsweek,* 12 February 2001, 40–43.

Chapter 18: The Ultimate Standard of Care: Faithfulness: God's Litmus Test

1. See G. A. Seefeldt and E. C. Roehlkepartain, "Tapping the Potential: Discovering [the] Congregation's Role in Building Assets in Youth," Search Institute Brochure, Minneapolis, Minnesota, 1998.

Moody Press, a ministry of Moody Bible Institute,
is designed for education, evangelization, and edification.
If we may assist you in knowing more about Christ
and the Christian life, please write us without obligation:
Moody Press, c/o MLM, Chicago, Illinois 60610.

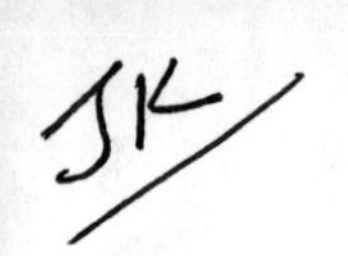